deliberate
————————●*[adj.]*

OVERCOME THE OVERWHELM
AND
RECLAIM YOUR BREATHING ROOM

RELEVANT PAGES PRESS

Published by Relevant Pages Press, Charleston, South Carolina.

Scripture quotations are taken from the following biblical translations:

Scripture taken from the New King James Version®. Copyright © 1982 by Thomas Nelson. Used by permission. All rights reserved.

Scripture quotations taken from the New American Standard Bible® (NASB), copyright © 1960, 1962, 1963, 1968, 1971, 1972, 1973, 1975, 1977, 1995 by The Lockman Foundation. Used by permission, www.Lockman.org

Scripture quotations are taken from the Holy Bible, New Living Translation, copyright ©1996, 2004, 2007, 2013, 2015 by Tyndale House Foundation. Used by permission of Tyndale House Publishers, Inc., Carol Stream, Illinois 60188. All rights reserved.

Scriptures taken from the Holy Bible, New International Version®, NIV®. Copyright © 1973, 1978, 1984, 2011 by Biblica, Inc.™ Used by permission of Zondervan. All rights reserved worldwide. www.zondervan.com. The "NIV" and "New International Version" are trademarks registered in the United States Patent and Trademark Office by Biblica, Inc.™

Scripture quotations are from the ESV® Bible (The Holy Bible, English Standard Version®), copyright © 2001 by Crossway, a publishing ministry of Good News Publishers. Used by permission. All rights reserved.

Scripture quotations marked MSG are taken from THE MESSAGE, copyright © 1993, 1994, 1995, 1996, 2000, 2001, 2002 by Eugene H. Peterson. Used by permission of NavPress. All rights reserved. Represented by Tyndale House Publishers, Inc.

Scripture quotations are from Revised Standard Version of the Bible, copyright © 1946, 1952, and 1971 National Council of the Churches of Christ in the United States of America. Used by permission. All rights reserved worldwide.

Cover and interior layout by Betts Keating Design.
Author photo: Elizabeth Koziatek

ISBN: 978-1-947303-22-5
Library of Congress Control Number: 2017958089

Printed in the United States of America.

*Thank you to my soul mate and husband, Jay,
for standing with me through the roller
coaster of my crazy amazing career.
You've always encouraged me to write a book.
Well babe, by the grace of God, it's finally here.*

*This book is dedicated
to everyone who wants to break
free from the overwhelm
and have more time to breathe.*

deliberate

adjective [dih-lib-er-it][1]

1.

done consciously and intentionally

'a deliberate attempt to reconcile the situation'

2.

careful and unhurried

'a conscientious and deliberate worker'

> **2.1 Fully considered and not impulsive**
> 'a deliberate decision'

contents

Introduction:
Welcome to the *deliberate* Tribe! 9

Chapter 1:
Purge Your Patterns 17

Chapter 2:
Make Peace with Imperfection 47

Chapter 3:
Break Up with Control 77

Chapter 4:
Ditch the Distracted Mind 109

Chapter 5:
Get Serious About Breathing Room 139

Chapter 6:
Grow Deeper with God 173

Sending Forth:
My Prayer for Your Continuing Journey 203

Acknowledgments 207

Notes 211

About the Author 213

welcome
to the deliberate tribe!

If you're like me, you might be tempted to skip the first few pages and get right into the meat. After all, you're busy. You barely have time to read a book, let alone the introduction.

That's exactly why I hope you'll stick with me. You don't have time to waste.

The few minutes you invest to learn more about *deliberate* will help you hit the ground running. Sure, I'll tell you a little bit about my journey. It's good context for the path ahead. But most importantly, my goal is to jump-start your journey.

Join me for a chat. And let's do this deliberate thing together.

deliberate Q&A

What is the passion behind the book?

I am passionate about *deliberate* because I want to help people break free from the self-perpetuated lifestyle of "busy" that is so prevalent in our culture today. When we're constantly busy—when we're always striving for more, different, or better—it's easy to get distracted by insignificant things that ultimately crowd out God's significance. I also sense many of us live complex, inauthentic lives based on what the world tells us is important, when we really desire the simplicity of living more peacefully in our own skin. I've tasted the freedom that comes when I stop pursuing end-games that don't satisfy and instead start living for what matters most. Many people are stressed out and maxed out, and I pray these short hope-full lessons help to offer a way out.

What's the back story?

I have spent most of my adult years working in the corporate world. Yet, for part of that time, my spirit and soul were dying there.

I call 2007 the year of crash and burn. My work schedule had become excruciating. I was traveling for business way more than was healthy for me. Add to that an over-committed calendar and an over-full task list, and you get the recipe for complete burnout: too many "yesses" (both inside and outside of work) and zero boundaries, mixed with only a tiny drop of downtime. My self-care was suffering and my ability to care well for others wasn't too far behind.

I often labeled my existence as a stressed-out "prison of overwhelm" and I had no idea how to escape. Even the mere thought of orchestrating an escape was overwhelming. I felt like the only way to break free was to do something drastic like quit my job and start over. But my reality didn't accommodate drastic. I have family. I had binding business commitments. And I wasn't in a financial or life position to just drop everything and run away. Even though I fantasized about it. A LOT.

Thing is, even though I was crazy busy, finding ways to feed my soul (and being intentional to exercise) helped me maintain what little healthy perspective I had. I listened to inspirational music while driving. I watched favorite TV preachers in my hotel room while preparing to visit a client site. I'd cut out and tape copies of scriptures to the inside of my travel folders. I'd read great "soul food" books during my airplane rides. And when I had a chance to run, I'd either run in meditative silence or listen to my favorite praise and worship tunes (mixed with classic rock 'n' roll, of course).

Through these splashes of God-infused time, I started to gain more clarity on why my life was a blur. I started to own the reality that I was the author of my own complexity, and my prison of overwhelm was largely built by me. Trying to be perfect. Trying to control outcomes. Trying to control what clients, friends, and family thought of me. Trying to please everyone. Trying to hold fast to my identity as a successful and knowledgeable consultant. Trying. Trying. Trying. Which led to doing. Doing. Doing.

One specific Saturday in September 2007, all my years of trying and doing came together to bring me to my knees–literally. I was leading major projects for multiple clients, as well as managing several sub-contractors who were helping me to get the jobs done. I had worked late Friday night and got up at 5 a.m. Saturday to meet one project deadline while preparing to leave town again on Sunday in support of another one. Sandwiched in between was a family breakfast on Saturday morning to celebrate my dad's birthday. I didn't know at the time, but it was the last birthday we'd celebrate with him before he passed away.

I remember that day like it was yesterday. Prior to leaving for Dad's birthday breakfast, I fell to my knees on the bathroom floor and cried out (with my husband as a witness): "I can't do this anymore."

I am not a drama queen and I have zero patience for drama. But, ironically, it was in that moment of surrender that something shifted. I turned the corner. Little did I know, but I began the *deliberate* journey. At the time, I didn't have a name for it. But eventually, in 2011, I began writing about it via newsletter as "Narrow Gate Nuggets," based on my heart for the scriptures Matthew 7:13-14:

Enter through the narrow gate. For wide is the gate and broad is the road that leads to destruction, and many enter through it. But small is the gate and narrow the road that leads to life, and only a few find it.

In this passage from Jesus' Sermon on the Mount, Jesus explained that the road to true life in him is a narrow one. In the spirit of that context, I believe God used these verses to show me a way out from the overwhelm by inspiring a new level of intention in my decision making.

Over time, this idea of choosing a life-giving narrow path became embedded into the depths of my mind, body and soul. As I kept writing about it through the nuggets, and as I experienced positive changes in my stress level, I realized I was making progress. The more I chose to refocus my mental and physical energies toward God and his truth—and the more I chose to release wide path patterns like fear, perfection, control, and over-achieving—the more I began to reset my priorities and restore healthy balance in my life. It wasn't easy, but it also wasn't rocket science. It happened *one decision at a time.* The more mindful I became, even with the smallest choice, the more I began to move the needle and break free from the overwhelm. The bonus: the more I broke free, the more I began to unleash an extreme trust in God in all things—both the big and the little.

I often say this book is common sense. It's full of stuff you might already know, written by someone you probably don't. At the same time, I am grateful for the authors I've read who took the time to share their hearts and write their stories... because I know, sometimes, I need to hear other people's experiences before my own common sense kicks in.

Yes, the book is finished, but my journey continues. I don't have it all figured out, and for that reason I am on the deliberate path *with* you. I hope and pray that the lessons in this book inspire you to do a few things differently and find more peace and presence in your crazy busy life. Deliberately.

What can I expect in reading it?

Think of *deliberate* as a nutrition-packed protein shake, not a five-course meal. While I hope you chew on the broader messages, the goal of each lesson is to pack a lot of nourishment into as few words as possible so it goes down easy and gets into your system fast.

deliberate is not a self-help book; it's a "help me God" journey. It's a practice that needs to be lived out indefinitely in the changing seasons of life. It requires courage to do things differently, and it requires cultivating greater trust in God to stay the course. In fact, if you're looking for a magic pill to fix your overwhelm, you might want to give this book to a friend, re-sell it on Amazon, or donate it to the library. It's not for everyone. But if you're looking for a manageable read to help move the needle on the amount of stress you accept into your life, then come along for the ride with an open heart and see what God has in store.

How is *deliberate* structured?

- Each chapter begins with a page of quotes to support the chapter theme, followed by six "Lessons."

- Lessons 1-5 each include a "Test It" and a "Trust It" opportunity:

   - **Test It:** Suggestions for reflection and small, but potentially significant, ways to practice each lesson within the scope of your daily life.

° **Trust it:** Scriptures to build your faith and inspire greater trust in God. (All scriptures are from the New International Version (NIV) of the Bible unless otherwise noted.)

• In the spirit of the Sabbath, the final lesson in the chapter invites you to simply "Rest" in a scripture after reading the lesson.

• Finally, each chapter concludes with a "Lessons Learned" page that summarizes key points. (Note: I always encourage writing notes in the body of the book to record any personal lessons learned during your reading.)

• Don't forget the back of the book. In addition to the usual stuff like Acknowledgments, etc., you'll find a "Sending Forth" prayer to encourage and strengthen you as you walk out *deliberate* in your daily life.

Is it a devotional book or a group discussion book?

Yes and yes! The *deliberate* journey can be a book or an experience – or a little bit of both! A few thoughts:

• **Personal devotional** – read with your coffee, in a waiting room, on the commuter train, in the airport, on an airplane, while waiting to pick up the kids at school...whenever it works in your schedule. (And the bathroom counts, too!)

• **The BFF approach** – share with a close friend or family member and journey together.

• **Casual discussion groups** – gather a few friends and do *deliberate* in broader community, like a book club.

- **Formal discussion groups** – use in church small groups or in workplace prayer/study groups if available.

If you want to amp up your journey, experience *deliberate* as a "Boot Camp" – either personally or in a group setting.

Here's how.

- Set a six-week timeline for your boot camp.

- Focus on one chapter each week.

- Read one lesson per day for six days. Practice the "Trust it" exercises and write down your reflections. (Discuss with your group, if applicable.)

- Rest on the seventh day.

- If you miss a day, or miss an exercise, no worries! Life happens. Simply pick it up the next day or next week and jump back in. You've got this!

What's with the *deliberate* Tribe?

If you are reading this book, you belong to an adventurous community who wants more God, more breathing room, and more peace in your daily life. Everyone is welcome in the tribe—no matter where you are in your faith walk. Join the conversation at www.deliberatetribe.com.

a word of caution

For those of us who are hard-wired as perfectionists, there is danger in the deliberate: we might find ourselves wanting to be perfect in our journey. I'll take you off the hook right now. The deliberate life is about growth and progress, not about perfection. Letting go of perfect is part of our journey to overcoming the overwhelm, and I look forward to doing that with you.

Now, let's go rock it!

purge your patterns

If you do what you've always done,
you'll always get what you've always gotten.
Anthony Robbins

Until you take responsibility for your decisions and
resulting actions, you will always be looking for
a scapegoat to blame for your problems.
You and I are responsible for our choices.
John Maxwell

Change your choices, change your life.
Tommy Newberry

Intentionality is the singular realm in our lives
over which we have complete control.
France de Sales

Every wall is a door.
Ralph Waldo Emerson

hitting the wall

DEVELOP AWARENESS OF YOUR DEFAULTS

As we journey together on the *deliberate* path, you'll quickly learn I don't have it all figured out. You'll also learn God uses my everyday experiences to teach me the value of slowing down and living more mindfully.

I remember one teaching moment I experienced while tidying the house. By force of habit, I was on a mindless quest to eliminate visible clutter. At tornado-like speed, I grabbed something from the living room table and spun around to go towards the kitchen. I can't tell you exactly what I grabbed, but I can tell you what happened next: I hit the wall. Literally.

I wish I could say I wasn't used to the floor plan. Or better yet, I had my eyes closed and couldn't see where I was going. But alas, the fact remains I hit the wall. Square on my nose, eyes wide open. My husband Jay was a witness so I couldn't even pretend it didn't happen.

I only got a small bruise from the mishap. Thankfully, I also got a revelation about doing life: What if, instead of viewing our walls as barriers to progress, we view them as doors to *awareness*– an invitation to slow down, look up, and be intentional to think about where we're headed next?

I don't know about you, but in my pursuit of escaping the overwhelm, I've hit the figurative wall many times. Even though I've read excellent books that marked me...listened to wise leaders who influenced me...and made process changes that helped streamline my busyness...I still couldn't get unstuck from the lifestyle of doing. In fact, there were times when my checklist of new ways to find balance became so heavy I felt even more overwhelmed.

Then one day, just like hitting that wall, I hit on a new reality that changed my thinking. I considered maybe the first step to getting unstuck from the lifestyle of busy was less about finding new ideas and more about identifying and purging the unhealthy default patterns that contributed to my overwhelm.

For example, saying "yes" to too many commitments without considering the broader impact. Or randomly checking email because it's there. Or mindlessly tidying clutter that really didn't make or break the value of the day.

These patterns look different for all of us, but I believe they get so deeply woven into our fabric we don't often stop and think about what we're doing and why. Yet, if we did, we might make different choices regarding how we invest our time.

My friends, awareness is the first step to change. When you hit the wall, be encouraged! Embrace the opportunity to slow down, look up, and think about where you're headed next... one decision at a time.

test it

———————○———————

The process to purge unhealthy default patterns is not for the faint of heart. It takes practice, patience, perseverance and, of course, prayer.

Think about it: Where in your life do you feel stuck in busyness, like you're hitting the wall? Instead of viewing that wall as a negative, consider how it may invite you to slow down and consider a different path.

my notes

_____

_____

_____

_____

_____

_____

_____

_____

_____

_____

_____

trust it

———————————◦———————————

Be very careful, then, how you live –
not as unwise but as wise.
Ephesians 5:15

the unmade bed

Early in my journey toward changing my default patterns, I chose to do something dramatic:

I left my bed unmade.

Now, for some of you, there's no drama in that choice. BUT we all have a thing—or two or three. For me, as a self-employed consultant who works at home, any bit of disorder around the house can send me reeling—including an unmade bed. "Cluttered space, cluttered mind" is my mantra. Even though there's healthy truth in that, I'll be the first to admit forcing myself to do certain chores each day is borderline obsessive.

So, guess what? I left the bed unmade one day...and the world did not come crashing down.

Yes, there was tension. Every time I saw that bed, I cringed. It felt messy. It felt irresponsible. It felt unorganized. It felt weird. It was different than my normal routine. Yet, it was also eye-opening. The lessons I learned in that one small choice increased my self-awareness in two profound ways.

One, I realized I have a hard time letting go—even of the little things. I'm sure it has something to do with my history of perfectionism and a need for control. After all, making my bed is not a bad thing and I can control whether or not I do it. On that day, I chose not to. I chose to let it go. The freedom I felt in that small decision provided a broader revelation—I could let go of something and life still worked.

Two, it reminded me how easy it is to get distracted in my "doing" of default routines—checking the proverbial box on the many little tasks on my list, and not stopping to consider the choices I'm making and what's behind them. At the end of the day, I know if my default routine consistently rules, I leave little room for spontaneity, and I might miss enjoying and appreciating the things in life that feed my heart and soul.

While I still make my bed on most days, I now do it from a place of freedom. Not because I feel obligated to make the bed, but because I mindfully choose to.

When it comes to bringing awareness to our default patterns, every choice can teach us something. Let's start with something small, and let's start today!

test it

———○———

Baby steps over time add up to meaningful changes.

Identify one of your "unmade beds" – something you are borderline obsessed with doing on a regular basis. Whether it's a chore at home or a non-mission critical task at work, choose to leave it undone for a reasonable period of time. How does it make you feel, and what do you think is behind that feeling? (e.g. perfection, control, guilt, people-pleasing, etc.) Pick something else, and repeat. How can you apply these learnings to other decisions in your life?

my notes

_____

_____

_____

_____

_____

_____

_____

_____

_____

_____

trust it

—————————————————○—————————————————

*As Jesus and his disciples were on their way,
he came to a village where a woman named Martha
opened her home to him. She had a sister called
Mary, who sat at the Lord's feet listening to what he said.
But Martha was distracted by all the preparations that had
to be made. She came to him and asked, "Lord, don't you
care that my sister has left me to do the work by myself?
Tell her to help me!"*

*"Martha, Martha," the Lord answered, "you are worried and
upset about many things, but few things are needed–
or indeed only one. Mary has chosen what is better, and it
will not be taken away from her."*
Luke 10:38-42

the art of opposite

PRACTICE DIFFERENT DECISIONS

I still enjoy watching re-runs of the TV show Seinfeld when I need a little comedic brain candy.

If you know the series, you might recall the episode, "The Opposite."[2] The character George Costanza decided that, to change outcomes in his life for the positive, he had to deliberately make decisions the opposite of what he would normally do. The result? He eventually got a new girlfriend, a dream job with the New York Yankees, and finally moved out of his parents' house.

What I love about this episode is the parallel to how we can make meaningful changes in our own lives by stepping back and practicing the *art of opposite* when it comes to overcoming default patterns.

In my own journey, I've practiced being Opposite Kathy in several areas related to my business.

For one, I practice "parking" business and personal development opportunities, instead of acting on them right away for FOMO (Fear of Missing Out). Believe me, this one's hard because

I get bored quickly. I enjoy trailblazing, creating, and learning. I can testify, however, that when I take a moment (or a month) to take a breath and consider the pros and cons of an opportunity, I grow my trust in God and have seen how he will reveal the best investments of my time at the right time.

I also practice putting boundaries around answering non-urgent emails and texts, instead of defaulting to immediately respond when they hit the inbox. I'm not sure what induces that self-imposed pressure to respond right away, but it's something at the intersection of perfection, control, and worrying about what others think of me—none of which fuel the deliberate life.

As Opposite Kathy, I practice refining my definition of productivity, no longer defaulting to "more is better" when it comes to planning my days. Most of all, I practice re-training my brain to focus less on my undone tasks and *more on what God has done for me.*

The beauty of practicing Opposite Kathy with my unhealthy defaults is that it opens the door to Authentic Kathy—a human being who can live more freely as God created her to be.

Yes, I still have my default days. Plenty of them. After all, life is not a sitcom and most of our goals don't manifest in 30 minutes like they did for George Costanza. But by the unfailing grace of God, I am learning to view my choices as options rather than obligations, which opens the door to a greater number of mindful decisions. I am progressing from being an over-committed perfectionist to becoming a fully committed peace-seeker—a woman who is learning to let go of striving and yearning to trust God even more.

test it

———————○———————

When we get out of our comfort zones to make certain opposite decisions toward our deliberate lives, over time we'll discover it becomes one of the most precious places to know and trust God on a deeper level.

In what area of your life could you benefit most from practicing the art of opposite? Now practice being Opposite George in that area for the next day or two. (Yes, it does take practice!) Ask the Lord (often) to give you strength as you learn to do some things differently.

my notes

_____

_____

_____

_____

_____

_____

_____

_____

_____

trust it

―――――――――○―――――――――

For my thoughts are not your thoughts,
neither are your ways my ways,"
declares the Lord.
"As the heavens are higher than
the earth, so are my ways higher
than your ways and my
thoughts than your thoughts."
Isaiah 55:8 – 9

the math problem

As with most perfectionistic people-pleasers, I am an enthusiastic "yes" girl by default. Therefore, choosing to say "no" was (and still is) one the greatest challenges I face in practicing the art of opposite—especially when it comes to declining good and noble opportunities.

I vividly remember the angst I felt the first time I declined a volunteer opportunity at our current church. My internal dialogue went something like this: "What will people think of you for not doing this?" said my longtime, imaginary friend, Ms. I-Have-To-Do-It-All. Of course, she added emphatically, "You are weak. What is wrong with you? Other people are just as busy, if not busier, than you. You *should* do this. After all, it's *church*!"

I'm sharing my dialogue to empathize with you. If you find it hard to say no to good and noble things, you're not alone. The struggle is real.

Here's the other reality: every "yes" in our lives is a "no" to something else...or someone else. It's a trade-off, no matter how we look at it. And what are we trading off? Physical and spiritual health? Precious energy? Valuable time? Important relationships? Opportunities for self-care?

The deal is, because we don't flex our "no" muscles enough, we wind up on the losing side of a math problem: we add more stuff to our lives than we subtract. I think we all know how that equation ends—a big fat zero. Zero time for God. Zero time for family and friends. Zero time for self-care. Zero time to simply rest and be still.

Correcting the math problem won't happen overnight. We didn't wake up one day suddenly busy, and chances are we won't wake up suddenly free from the things that overwhelm us. But we can begin to tip the scales in our favor by trading our automatic "yes" for a mindful "yes" or a deliberate "no." Except for the extenuating circumstances in our lives, either we manage our calendar or our calendar manages us. We have a choice.

Having the courage to flex my "no" muscles has allowed me to make progress in living less busy. I'm not there yet and probably won't get there this side of heaven. But the more I press on, the more breathing room I experience with each passing season. And while I do volunteer for certain opportunities in my church, I do it enthusiastically and willingly...not because I feel guilty or obligated.

Counter to what popular culture wants you to believe, activity does not determine your value. God did not create you to be busy all the time—even at church. He loves peace, and he promises perfect peace to those who remain steadfast in him and his truth— not steadfast in activity.

test it

○

Flexing our "no" muscles in the face of something good is hard, but sometimes it's the healthiest and most mature decision.

Next time you are tempted to give an automatic "yes" because you think you should say yes, step back and consider: "If I add this commitment, what am I trading off? Is it worth the sacrifice—both now and over the longer term? Do I really have the time or am I creating a math problem?"

my notes

trust it

─────────────○─────────────

*You will keep in perfect peace those whose
minds are steadfast, because they trust in you.*
Isaiah 26:3

the MacNugget

Not too long ago, I decided to improve efficiency in my business infrastructure to better manage the multiple hats that go with being self-employed, as well as with juggling my other life roles. A major step in that direction came when, after 25 years in a Microsoft Windows environment, I switched my computer platform to Apple Mac.

I quickly discovered that this transition for efficiency's sake was temporarily inefficient, because I had to re-train myself and learn to interact with my computer in a whole new way.

On one of my more frustrated days, after I surrendered myself to being a defeated old dog who couldn't learn new tricks, my hubby shared some words of wisdom. "Don't be so hard on yourself," he said. "You're not just learning something new, you're having to un-learn the old way of doing things."

Bam.

Suddenly, the weight was lifted. I believe God used my husband to speak life to my soul. Instead of feeling defeated, I felt touched by grace, realizing I was fully capable of learning this new thing. Sure, the old Windows habits didn't die easily. Yet, after several weeks on the new Mac, my new normal began flowing more naturally.

I hope this experience provides encouragement: If you get frustrated as you attempt to purge your default patterns and flex your "no" muscles, you're not alone. Remember, coming unstuck from the overwhelm requires practice, patience, perseverance, and prayer. It also requires a healthy dose of self-compassion. The deliberate life *is an ongoing process*, not a final destination. As you take this journey, be sure to give yourself the same compassion and encouragement you'd give a friend.

Even when we can't see it right away, we will eventually look back and see how God's grace met us in the middle of our undoing and unlearning. Tribe, you can do this deliberate thing. Go for it and grow through it. With God, anything is possible!

test it

It takes time to loosen our grip on unhealthy patterns. Don't beat yourself up if you don't get it right every time. There really is no right and wrong, only progress.

Next time you find yourself struggling to sustain a new habit or behavior, encourage yourself out loud, as you would a good friend. It might sound silly, but if you stay with it you will gradually learn to replace negative self-talk with greater self-compassion.

my notes

trust it

The Lord is gracious and compassionate.

Psalm 111:4

a matter of thinking

Sometimes we choose to change.

Sometimes change chooses us.

Living in the St. Louis area, I'm reminded of that whenever we experience a major tornado. Obviously, tornado victims have change forced upon them in a matter of seconds. Yet, I am always humbled by their spirit. When they're interviewed on TV, they will talk less about what they've lost and more about how thankful they are their lives were spared. Their homes lie in complete wreckage, but their focus is on gratitude.

Granted, the deliberate journey is not a natural disaster that is forced upon us. It's a change we're choosing. But like those tornado victims, we have a choice on where to focus.

As life spins around us...

As the world tells us more is better...

As we have more opportunities coming our way than
we do time...

Things get blurry. Before we know it, our deliberate journey
turns into a distracted journey and our focus is distorted. And
let's face it, what we focus on tends to expand in significance.

If we focus too much on our fears, they become bigger
than our faith.

If we focus too much on our problems, they become
bigger than our possibilities.

If we focus too much on our trials, they become bigger
than our trust.

If we even focus too much on our gifts, they become
bigger and more prominent than our Giver.

Friends, we are not pursuing the deliberate life out of selfish
ambition or to achieve some ideal of perfect. Yes, there is a
self-care component to living deliberately that we'll cover later
in the book. But the deliberate life is not a self-absorbed life;
it's a God-absorbed life. *It is a God-focused life.*

My prayer for you, as a one-of-a-kind member of the
deliberate Tribe, is that you find a new level of focus on God
alone! He does not want you to continue this lifestyle of being
too overwhelmed to truly enjoy your life. Even on days when
you don't feel God is near, get into your heart space and stand
on the truth: God is *for* you, he is drawing near to you and his
love for you *never* fails.

rest

I keep my eyes always on the Lord.
With him at my right hand,
I will not be shaken.
Psalm 16:8

purge your patterns

- Hitting the wall is an invitation to slow down, look up, and think about where you're headed next. The wall is not a barrier to progress, but rather a door to awareness and an opportunity to choose a different path.

- Every choice you make, even the small ones, can teach you something about your default patterns. If your defaults rule your life on a regular basis, you leave little room for spontaneity and might miss enjoying and appreciating the things in life that feed your heart and soul.

- Practicing the art of opposite with your unhealthy defaults can help you live more freely as God created you to be. Viewing your choices as options instead of obligations opens the door to a greater number of mindful decisions.

- Every "yes" in your life is a "no" to something else or someone else. It's a tradeoff, no matter how you look at it. Except for the extenuating circumstances in your life, either you manage your calendar or your calendar manages you.

- Practice self-compassion. The deliberate journey is a process. When things get tough, give yourself the same compassion and encouragement you'd give a friend.

- The deliberate life is a God-focused life, and where you focus matters.

make peace with imperfection

The thing that is really hard and really amazing is giving up on being perfect and beginning the work of becoming yourself.
Anna Quindlen

Embracing ourselves has nothing to do with arrogance or settling for a lower version of who we are. Embracing ourselves has everything to do with embracing the goodness of God's creative work in us. It means trusting God, believing that all he has made is glorious and good. And that includes us. You are the only one who can be you.
Stasi Eldredge

Comparison is the thief of joy.
Theodore Roosevelt

Masterpieces aren't made by run-of-the-mill craftsmen; they require the skilled hands of a genius. They are one-of-a-kind, never-to-be-repeated gifts to the world. And that's what you are, God's one-of-a-kind, never-to-be-repeated gift to the world.
Geri Scazzero

We please him most, not by frantically trying to make ourselves good, but by throwing ourselves into his arms with all our imperfections and believing that he understands everything and still loves us.
A.W. Tozer

wind chasers

---◇---

I was placing groceries in the car one day, and it happened: a gust of wind snatched the receipt sitting loosely on top of my bag and lofted it into the air. As a gal who started her own "Pollution Solutions" club in grade school, I make a point to pick up my litter. So, I earnestly pursued the receipt, desperately hoping I would not see myself on YouTube a few hours later as the crazy lady chasing paper across a parking lot.

Thankfully, I retrieved it quickly. More thankfully, God used that moment to remind me of one of my favorite scriptures, Ecclesiastes 4:6:

Better one handful with tranquility than two handfuls with toil and chasing after the wind.

When it comes to how we do life these days, I believe we've generally become a culture of wind chasers. Professionally. Parentally. Socially. Materially. You name it.

In pursuit of what we think will be the perfect life, we end up making our lives more complex.

We say "yes" to too many things.

We define success through worldly things.

We measure our value by accomplishing to-do list things.

We toil to the point where we're carrying more than two handfuls of stuff on our plate, then we wonder why we can't find tranquility in anything. Toiling takes a lot of time, not to mention energy.

Our pastor has often said, "There is no 'there' there." In other words, we chase achievements and experiences and things, thinking once we get "there," then life will be heaven on earth. But just as we can't catch the wind, we can't catch perfect. Rather, we find the satisfaction of "there" is temporary, and the cycle starts all over again. Chasing the perfect life is exhausting.

What would it look like to make peace with imperfection and pursue tranquility through a one-handful life of moderation—in our commitments, our things, and our to-do lists? What would it look like if, instead of chasing the perfect life, we spent more time chasing after a deeper knowledge of our perfect God?

test it

In our culture that dictates more is better, a one-handful life of moderation doesn't come naturally.

What does one-handful living look like to you? What "wind" are you chasing to attain some ideal of perfect and what is it costing you? Identify it. If you journal, journal it. Either way, ask yourself: What one decision can I make differently today to stop chasing perfect? Be on the lookout for opportunities to practice that decision.

my notes

trust it

---○---

*I have seen that every labor and every
skill which is done is the result of
rivalry between a man and his neighbor.
This too is vanity and striving after
wind; One hand full of rest is better
than two fists full of labor
and striving after wind.*
Ecclesiastes 4:4, 6 NASB

the gift of imperfection

ACCEPT THE INVITATION TO REST

Even though I have struggled with default patterns of perfectionism, I've always had a soft heart for imperfect things —the ugly pumpkin, the "Charlie Brown" Christmas tree, and the ugly puppy, just to name a few. (Though, personally, I think *all* puppies are cute.)

I'm not sure exactly why I have a soft heart for this stuff, but I imagine there's something about these imperfect things that gives me hope. After all...

The ugly pumpkin can still be a jack-o-lantern on the porch at Halloween. The Charlie Brown Christmas tree can still bring joy to someone's home over the holidays. And the ugly puppy can still give lots of love to his human family. Friends, therein lies the hope: all of these imperfect things still have value, and their imperfection is part of their story. Yet, we spend a lot of precious time trying to erase imperfection from our stories.

There are many reasons behind that, depending on where we struggle personally with imperfection. Regardless, I think the media plays a huge role in contributing to our struggle. We are constantly bombarded by advertising and TV shows that feed our ideal of the picture-perfect life. Then, often by default, we find ourselves investing time, energy, and resources to erase our imperfection and attain some version of picture-perfect–the perfect house, the perfect backyard, the perfect kids, the perfect vacation, the perfect dinner party.

The pursuit of perfect keeps us busy and adds to our overwhelm. It keeps us in a cycle of striving where we habitually over-effort to do more or have more, because we have come to believe that who we are or what we have isn't enough by picture-perfect standards.

To make peace with our imperfect lives, I believe we need a huge paradigm shift:

Instead of viewing imperfection as a call to action, let's *receive* imperfection as an invitation to rest–a gift that allows us to stop striving for the picture-perfect life and start living with a new level of contentment.

In our current season.

Where we are.

With what we have.

In our own skin.

Only God is perfect. While I aspire to live well, I can't be God. I mess up a lot. Yet, the beauty of it all is the Lord is writing my story despite my shortcomings. By viewing imperfection as an invitation to rest, I am learning God's grace will meet me in my weakness and that I am valuable, flaws and all!

test it

Viewing imperfection as an invitation to rest can be a huge paradigm shift in the deliberate journey.

Observe your patterns of striving this week. Which ones are driven by pursuit of the picture-perfect life, one in which you are trying to cover or over compensate for flaws? How can you take one small step of faith to release striving in that area?

my notes

trust it

He has made everything
beautiful in its time.
Ecclesiastes 3:11

lessons by candlelight

―――――――――――――――――○―――――――――――――――――

APPRECIATE YOUR AUTHENTICITY

There's something about candles and Christmas that go together. So, when I led a special Christmas event at a local church, I knew immediately I wanted to use candlelight. Of course, I wanted it to be perfect.

As things were rolling in that season of life, I had waited until the last minute to pull the candles together. About two hours before go-time, I went to the basement. I began counting the candles I had in storage for these types of events. I considered the size of the room. It was then that Captain Obvious hit me: I didn't have enough candles to fully light the space without using electricity.

Moving into action mode (my default at the time), I grabbed the storage bin of battery-operated candles. Then I scurried upstairs and gathered all the random candles in my home.

When I finally had everything in one place, my perfectionism rose and my heart sank: All I saw was an imperfect hodgepodge of candles that didn't match.

My first thought was a rush visit to the store to buy all new candles. But because I was making progress to be mindful of my defaults, I moved on to my second thought. I considered the cost of seeking perfection—namely the added expense on my tight budget, as well as the added hurry to an already hectic day.

Alas, I chose to let go of perfection and light the room with my hodgepodge of candles. In that choice, I believe God opened my heart-door to reveal an important lesson: *Even if every single candle is different, each one has a role to play in bringing light to the darkness.* Every. Candle. Matters.

Tribe, thankfully God does not view all of us as a hodgepodge of unmatched candles. He created each of us in his image to be unique beings, with our own individual gifts and imperfections. You have an assignment. I have an assignment. And we all have a role to play in lighting the world around us. When we choose to embrace that truth, we begin to appreciate our authenticity in new and powerful ways—imperfections and all.

test it

In God's eyes, we are loved and adored for who we are...
and we are called to love others in their imperfections
as well.

When has your focus on imperfection cost you
something (time, money, relationships, etc.)? When
has your focus on someone else's imperfections cost
you something? What is one small shift you can make
in your actions or thinking to help you better accept
imperfection in yourself and others?

my notes

_____

_____

_____

_____

_____

_____

_____

_____

_____

_____

trust it

─────────────────○─────────────────

I will give thanks to You, for I am fearfully
and wonderfully made; Wonderful are
Your works, and my soul knows it very well.
Psalm 139:14 NASB

finding the typos

———————◦———————

NURTURE THE GOOD STUFF

One of my friends is an executive coach and time management expert. She and I are author soul sisters because we both like to write short lessons that hopefully provide bigger *aha!* moments. When I first met her, she included the following disclaimer on her newsletters: *"Typos, if any, are here to make you feel good about finding them. You're welcome."*[3]

I love this. I even started to use it in emails with the clients I knew best. I also quit beating myself up for occasional typos, although it still stings when clients find them. It stings even more after I've invested significant time consolidating mounds of input into a concise message, and the first piece of feedback at the review meeting is about a typo on page 2. Seriously.

Yet, this is how we often roll in life. Whether it's typos in an email, weeds in the garden, or a spot on our favorite shirt. What is it about imperfection that gets our attention, even when we don't feel good about finding it?

The psychological answer to that question goes beyond my expertise. But even if I did know the textbook answer, my message would be the same: making peace with imperfection requires us to deliberately focus our energy on the good and positive things about ourselves and in our lives.

I almost hate writing that statement because it sounds so trite. The transformational "power of positive thinking" is nothing new. But let's face it: it's nearly impossible to have peace with our imperfect lives if we default to focusing on the negatives.

I'll admit, I struggle with this. While I'm not an expert in psychology, I *am* an expert at nurturing the negatives.

Before I published this book, I wrote "Narrow Gate Nuggets" via newsletter. In that time, I experienced the occasional and dreaded "un-subscriber." Even if I received ten positive messages about my writing, I focused all my mental energy—and then some—on the one person who dropped out. As I nurtured the negative, my brain got busy. I began to shrink back. I began thinking maybe I wasn't a good writer. Maybe I shouldn't be doing this.

Obviously, I am still writing, and I do still feel disappointed when people unsubscribe. Those two things co-exist. However, instead of nurturing the negative, which requires valuable energy, I use each un-subscriber as an opportunity to shift my focus to the positive feedback I have received. I have also come to realize that when people unsubscribe, it's not about my imperfection. It's more about where they are in their personal journey.

I believe one key to breaking free from the overwhelm lies in deliberately choosing to nurture the good stuff in our lives versus focusing on the negatives that keep our minds—and even our bodies—in a cycle of busy. We can use imperfection as an invitation to look higher and dwell in the truth that God loves us and has a great plan for each of us—regardless of our typos, weeds, and spots.

test it

A long-term shift in focus happens one opportunity at a time. We must be mindful of where we're investing our mental energy and what thoughts we decide to nurture.

What "typo" in your life occupies your brain space to the point where you: a) shrink back because you can't be perfect; or b) over-effort trying to be perfect? Even though it sounds cliché, be intentional to focus on the positive. For example, I began collecting happy feedback into one master document called "Good Vibes." When I find myself focusing on the negatives, I open my "Good Vibes" file for encouragement. (I also open my Bible and get some *God vibes!*)

my notes

trust it

———————○———————

Finally, brothers and sisters, whatever is true,
whatever is noble, whatever is right,
whatever is pure, whatever is lovely,
whatever is admirable—
if anything is excellent or praiseworthy—
think about such things.
Philipians 4:8

tale of the coffee grinder

GIVE UP COMPARISON

My husband Jay loves to do research on the internet. Any time we face a major (or even minor) purchase, the iPad comes out and Google comes up. With the click of the keyboard, we have tons of data at our fingertips. Personally, I love it when the web sites allow us to "check the box" and compare our potential choices against one another to find the perfect solution for our needs.

We thought we found perfection in a recent coffee grinder purchase. I should add we already had a fully functional coffee grinder, but we decided it didn't grind the coffee coarse enough for our French press. It was good, but not good enough. A first-world problem, I'll admit.

I'll also admit, once we started researching, we grew even more discontent with our current grinder and increasingly enamored by the more glamorous and capable grinders we discovered—one of which we eventually bought.

Fast forward: the new grinder was a bust. We sent it back. We are still using the original one. Not a life crisis by any means, but it does open the door to an interesting consideration: without the easy ability to compare our coffee grinder to others, we would not have known just how "imperfect" our grinder was. Ignorance can be bliss. Yet, we run into the same comparison trap when it comes to doing life: It's way too easy to compare ourselves.

We compare ourselves to others.

We compare ourselves to some ideal.

We compare ourselves to where we think we should be at our particular age.

We compare ourselves to what used to be back in the glory days of our youth—provided those were glory days, of course.

If we are constantly comparing ourselves to someone or something else—if we are constantly "shopping" for a certain version of perfect—the bliss of having peace with imperfection will continue to elude us. Comparison squashes our authenticity and kills our contentment, which opens the door to the overwhelm through over-doing, over-achieving, and over-consuming. There's no way to win at the comparison game. It either deflates you or inflates you. Neither outcome is God's best for you.

Let's lock arms, Tribe, and find greater peace with our imperfect lives by releasing comparison...one thought at a time.

test it

Comparison is a huge road block to making peace with imperfection.

What is your biggest struggle in this area? How does that struggle impact your behaviors, thought patterns, etc.? How can you begin to deliberately shift your focus away from comparison in this moment?

my notes

_____

_____

_____

_____

_____

_____

_____

_____

_____

_____

_____

_____

trust it

A heart at peace gives life to the body,
but envy rots the bones.
Proverbs 14:30

practice not perfect

Most of the lessons in *deliberate* come from my life experiences. This isn't one of them.

This lesson comes from my desire to be crystal clear about the path we're on to make peace with imperfection.

Specifically, in case this crossed your mind, I want to be clear I am not talking about a path of complacency where we say, "OK, I'm imperfect. It's not going to get any better than this, so I might as well have peace." Making peace with imperfection is not an excuse to curl up in a ball, ditch self-improvement, and become passive observers of our own lives.

Rather, making peace with our imperfect lives is an active journey that unfolds over time.

It's a luxurious opportunity to flex our "trust in God" muscles to work things out despite our flaws.

It's an exquisite calling to cultivate greater understanding and appreciation of how God values our individuality.

It's a magnificent exercise in resting with imperfection while at the same time becoming the best version of ourselves.

Oh, and it's not easy.

But there's one mantra that has helped me and I hope it helps you:

To find greater peace with imperfection, approach your life as a practice, not as a perfect.

One of my friends took this to heart when I shared it with her. She, in turn, encouraged me with a great example of how she lives it out practically:

She practices going to the gym. She practices not checking her cell phone with every little ding. She practices being still. She practices reading a devotional every morning. She practices healthy boundaries when it comes to leaving work on time.

Of course, my friend will be the first to tell you she doesn't get it right every day. But she will also tell you that her practice is resulting in progress. One day at a time, one decision at a time.

rest

———————————○———————————

*May the Lord smile on you and be
gracious to you. May the Lord show
you his favor and give you his peace.*
Numbers 6:25 – 26 NLT

make peace with imperfection

- Chasing the perfect life is exhausting. Just as you can't catch the wind, you can't catch perfect.

- Imperfection is an invitation to rest with where you are and in who you are—to stop striving for the picture-perfect life and start living with a new level of contentment.

- The deliberate life is lived by standing on the truth that you are uniquely and wonderfully made. When you choose to embrace that truth, you can begin to enjoy your authenticity in new and powerful ways—imperfections and all.

- Choose to nurture the good things in your life versus nurturing the negatives. Use imperfection as an opportunity to look higher and dwell in the truth that God loves you and has a great plan for you.

- Comparison squashes your authenticity and kills your contentment, which opens the door to the overwhelm through over-doing, over-achieving, and over-consuming.

- Approach life as a practice, not as a perfect. Not because practice makes perfect, but because practice results in progress.

break up with control

The only way God can show us he's in control
is to put us in situations we can't control.
Stephen Furtick

When I attempt to exercise control and power
I have strayed far from the embrace of the Father.
Pete Scazzero

One of the most arduous spiritual tasks
is that of giving up control and allowing
the Spirit of God to lead our lives.
Henri Nouwen

I used to think the opposite of control was chaos.
But it's not. The opposite of control is surrender.
Erin Loechner

Never be afraid to trust an unknown
future to a known God.
Corry Ten Boom

REST

---○---

DO YOUR PART AND LET GOD DO HIS

The older I get, the more I appreciate *mnemonics*. Now, before you roll your eyes and skip to Chapter 4, stick with me. The word looks complicated, but the concept is simple. Mnemonics are techniques that help aid our memory when it comes to recalling important information.

My go-to mnemonic is the use of acronyms. Basically, I use the first letter in a group of words to form a new word that helps me recall something specific. For example, if I need help remembering my grocery list during a spontaneous visit to the store, I might create the word "BETS"...which would remind me to buy: Bread. Eggs. Tomatoes. Salad greens.

Naturally, it's not a foolproof technique. Remembering the word is the easy part. Remembering what each letter represents is another story. Fortunately, however—more times than not—a little mnemonic goes a long way in helping me shop successfully.

To that end, as we continue our discussion of the deliberate life, I'm kicking off this chapter with a little mnemonic:

REST

Really... **E**nthusiastically... **S**top... **T**rying to *control everything*.

As a "believe it, achieve it" kind of gal when it comes to goals and dreams, I'm the first to admit REST doesn't come naturally—especially the enthusiastic part. Even though I'm wise enough to know I don't really control everything, there is still something comforting about the illusion of control—those unhealthy thoughts and actions that make me feel like I have control. Over-doing. Over-thinking. Over-worrying. Over-working. The list goes on.

Yes, to be good stewards of our lives, there are times when we need to manage what we can control (e.g. what we eat, what we say, how we spend our time, etc.). There are also times when we need to press on and persevere through life's challenges. I get that. I do that.

So, what does it mean to REST? I believe it means we cultivate a deliberate awareness to draw the line between doing our part and letting God do his part. REST is all about breaking up with control as we know it so we can fully receive the amazing gift of letting God be God. Really.

Friends, breaking up with our control patterns takes courage. It requires us to loosen our white-knuckle grip on our life as we think it should be. It requires us to live confidently as we pursue our dreams and goals, while at the same time remaining humble and remaining open to God's direction and detours.

When we take small steps to release our need to control, we will learn it's possible to find peace in the ongoing tension between the mind's need to figure it out and the soul's need to be still. When we become deliberate to REST, we begin to unleash an extreme trust in God that will grow the more we practice letting go.

test it

───────────────○───────────────

It takes self-reflection and ongoing discernment to have a healthy perspective on control.

How does the illusion of controlling outcomes contribute to your mental and/or physical overwhelm? Identify something in your life that brings out the control freak in you. Pray a simple prayer about it now. "God, I know I don't control this. I'm trusting you to work it out. Help me let it go." Keep this prayer close to your heart and repeat as necessary.

my notes

_____

_____

_____

_____

_____

_____

_____

_____

_____

_____

trust it

―――――――――○―――――――――

Come to me. Get away with me and you'll
recover your life. I'll show you how to take
a real rest. Walk with me and work with me—
watch how I do it. Learn the unforced rhythms
of grace. I won't lay anything heavy or
ill-fitting on you. Keep company with me
and you'll learn to live freely and lightly.
Matthew 11:28 – 30 The Message

control addict

RECOGNIZE HOW THE NEED FOR CONTROL
SHOWS UP IN YOUR LIFE

I remember one summer when Jay helped a friend-of-a-friend install a trailer hitch on her sport utility vehicle. At the time, this woman was a sales representative in the salon business. In appreciation, she gave us a generous bag full of high-end shampoos, conditioners, and other hair styling products. God is good in the little things, I'm just sayin'.

Of course, I eagerly unpacked that goodie bag like a child opening Christmas presents, and there was one product that immediately grabbed my attention: *"Control Addict"*—a maximum-hold hairspray that told me I could "get addicted to 24-hour control."

Since I love experimenting with new hair products, especially those that promise rock-star hair, I was all in. At the same time, this aptly-named hairspray reminded me how easy it is to get addicted to control in our own lives—without even realizing it.

Control addiction is sneaky. Over the years, I've seen how a perpetual need for control can creep into our behaviors under a variety of disguises.

It can show up as an over-abundance of *people pleasing*, where we seek approval by trying to control what others think of us.

It can show up as *anger* or *passive aggressive language*, where we use our words and/or actions to manipulate others to get what we want.

It can show up as unhealthy *isolation*, where we feel safer and more in control of our lives because we don't have to deal with the imperfect world and imperfect people around us.

It can even show up as *worry*, which doesn't accomplish anything but—for some reason—gives us a feeling of control over the future outcomes in our lives.

These potential manifestations of control addiction are just the tip of the iceberg. How it shows up for me and how it shows up for you may look completely different. No matter how it looks, however, the takeaway is the same:

A control-addicted life is *not* a deliberate life based on God's truths. It's a stressful life often rooted in some type of fear. (More on that later!)

While that Control Addict hairspray was totally awesome, being addicted to control is anything but. Releasing our need to control what we can't control is a big step in letting God be God.

test it

The need to control often manifests in our thoughts and actions.

How does control addiction disguise itself and show up in your life? What one small step can you take this week to take the pressure off yourself in that area...to do only your part and put greater trust in God to do his part?

my notes

trust it

―――――――――――――○―――――――――――――

Fear not, for I am with you; be not dismayed,
for I am your God; I will strengthen you,
I will help you, I will uphold
you with my righteous right hand.
Isaiah 41:10 ESV

the black sweater

---○---

If you've been on a God-journey for any length of time, chances are, "Let go and let God" is part of your faith vocabulary. However, even when we're 100 percent sincere about our intent to let go, saying it and doing it are two different things.

For me, this struggle of surrender often manifests itself in my closet...most recently with a favorite black sweater.

I got it at a resale shop so, aside from being something I enjoyed wearing, this sweater was a bargain. After a year or so, I began noticing small stress holes in the seam of the neckline. Thankfully, the design of the collar hid them. But then came the moth holes in the back of the sweater, which were impossible to hide. Yet, still determined to keep this garment, I resorted to wearing it exclusively around the house instead of in public.

Finally, after wearing it to the point of wearing it out, I decided it had to go. I struggled. *After all*, I thought, *What if I need it tomorrow? What if I can't find another one I like as much? What if our budget shrinks and I choose not to buy another one; maybe I should save this old sweater just in case?*

Bottom line, rational or not, my scarcity mentality had me fearing the outcome of releasing this piece of clothing.

Granted, it's a harmless example of holding on to something. But I believe the mental struggle with my sweater is exactly the type of struggle that keeps us from releasing control: *fear* of the outcome.

We fear being misunderstood.

We fear judgment.

We fear losing something or someone.

We fear failure.

We even fear success.

Even if it's subconsciously, we give more power to our fears than our faith. When that happens, we find ourselves placing more confidence in our own efforts to control life's outcomes than we are placing in God. On some level, I think we do that because we don't fully trust the Lord to work things out for us. That's hard to admit but, in our precious humanity, we have a hard time believing what we can't see.

Friends, letting go of control is not wimpy or passive. It's an active part of our faith walk that requires mindful decisions around our actions and behaviors. It's a season where we intentionally pursue an understanding of God's truth about our lives instead of living by our fears and the defeating feelings that go with them.

As we journey together to break up with control, I pray our trust in God becomes so outrageous that his perfect love casts out *all* fear! The struggle is real. Thankfully, so is God's grace.

test it

Fear is often at the root of our need for control. Yet, it's in the struggle of surrender that we can fully experience the security of our Savior.

In this season of life, what is your biggest fear when it comes to not being in control of an outcome? How is that fear contributing to any overwhelm you feel in your life? Take a couple minutes to Google a scripture about overcoming fear or use the one on the next page. Write it out and put it on a sticky note somewhere you will see it frequently. Be intentional to gaze at that scripture when your fears are driving you to a mindset of control.

my notes

_____

_____

_____

_____

_____

_____

_____

_____

_____

trust it

───────────────○───────────────

Be strong. Take courage. Don't be intimidated. Don't give them a second thought because God, your God, is striding ahead of you. He's right there with you. He won't let you down; he won't leave you.
Deuteronomy 31: 6 The Message

when control matters

USE SELF-CONTROL TO RELEASE CONTROL

Admittedly, I am one of those dog moms who adores my golden retriever as much as parents adore their children. I like to think, because he is a dog and I am a human, I have control over him. Of course, that's not the case.

Don't get me wrong; he is an awesome, well-behaved bundle of fur. However, sometimes when I ask him to come inside, he looks at me stubbornly and stays outside. Sometimes when we begin our morning walks, especially on hot days, he sits down at the end of the driveway and refuses to go. And almost every day, when he wants treats, he stands outside of my office whining ever-so-sweetly until I get up and give in.

Clearly, we know who's in control here. It's not me.

Thankfully, as a human being with the ability to live beyond instincts, I have one thing my dog doesn't: the discernment to *choose* self-control. Ironically, as we journey to break up with control as we know it, we need self-control to do it.

For example:

Self-control to set healthy boundaries in work
and relationships.

Self-control to recognize and stop excess in our work
and planning when we're doing it out of unhealthy motivation.

Self-control to release reputation management when we
are trying to control what others think of us.

Self-control to choose our words wisely so they are life-
giving and non-manipulative to others.

Self-control in our thought lives—choosing to dwell on
the promises of God rather than the worries and pressures
of our fears.

Self-control to get off the hamster wheel in our brains, being
mindful to do *less figuring out* and *more praying about.*

Self-control to realize enough is enough.

We have very little control over our pets, spouses, boyfriends, girlfriends, kids, friends, siblings, family, bosses, and co-workers, no matter how hard we try. But we can be mindful to step back and practice the gift of self-control. Like all tools in the deliberate tool box, self-control is a practice—it doesn't just happen. The good news: God's idea of self-control is not legalistic or restrictive; it is the path to true and meaningful freedom.

test it

Exercising self-control is essential to breaking up with control as we know it.

Where do you need to exercise greater self-control as you practice letting go of your need for control? Identify two doable changes in that area and commit to implementing them within the next week.

my notes

trust it

───────────────○───────────────

For God gave us a spirit not of fear
but of power and love and self-control.
2 Timothy 1:7 ESV

lessons from the birds

We have a large window at our kitchen sink. During the day, when I grab a glass of water, I often enjoy lingering for a moment and watching the birds. As they search for food in the ground or at the feeder, they seem to move about with carefree instinct and ease. We're convinced that one specific cardinal sits outside of our window just to let us know when the bird feeder is running low.

In those times, I love how God reminds me of a favorite scripture from Matthew:

Therefore I tell you, do not worry about your life, what you will eat or drink; or about your body, what you will wear. Is not life more than food, and the body more than clothes? Look at the birds of the air; they do not sow or reap or store away in barns, and yet your heavenly Father feeds them. Are you not much more valuable than they? Can any one of you by worrying add a single hour to your life? **(Matthew 6:25 – 27)**

While there's a lot of good stuff packed into these verses, the one thing I want to unpack relates to developing a greater trust in *God as our Provider*. Not a magic genie-type provider or a Santa Claus-type provider. But a supernatural provider who cares deeply about you and me.

Our provider of the opportunities that bring us income and employment.

Our provider of the material things we get to enjoy on this earth.

Our provider of cherished friends.

Our provider of comfort in tough times.

Our provider of physical and emotional healing.

Our provider of breakthroughs, in our lives and in loved ones' lives.

Just to be clear: God. Is. Our. Provider.

Yes, it's frustrating when things aren't happening as quickly as we'd like. Yes, it is hard to exercise our faith muscles and believe in what we can't see. In fact, depending on the situation, waiting for provision or breakthrough or healing can be downright scary. But life is even more scary if we view our mates, bosses, jobs, clients, government, doctors, even *ourselves* as providers. After all, people are fallible. We are fallible.

Instead of placing our faith in people as providers, let's place it in our Ultimate Provider. God's provision may look vastly different than what we expect, and sometimes we may not like the outcome. But that's when it takes digging down in our faith to rise above disappointment and root down in the Truth: God loves us unconditionally and promises to provide for our needs.

When we begin to stand on this truth and bury it in our hearts, I believe we stand on something that can radically change the way we do life. I believe it's something that can ultimately transform the busyness of control into a posture of surrender.

test it

───────────────○───────────────

Our view of provision will influence how busy we get trying to control things—both mentally and physically.

In which areas do you place more faith in people or yourself than in God to provide? What fear is behind that? Now, or next time you have an opportunity: Go to a window. Watch the birds. Take a breath. Remember the promise in Matthew 6:25 – 27. Say it out loud if you have it in front of you. Practice surrendering pieces of that fear and remind yourself that God is your Ultimate Provider.

my notes

_____

_____

_____

_____

_____

_____

_____

_____

_____

trust it

─────────────────○─────────────────

And my God will meet all your needs according to the riches of his glory in Christ Jesus.
Philippians 4:19

excess baggage

———○———

LEARN TO TRAVEL LIGHTLY

I have mastered the art of traveling heavy when I fly.

Specifically, I have been known to pack enough clothes and shoes for a 10-day trip in my carry-on suitcase and backpack. It's not because I enjoy lugging all that stuff around and gracefully (not) lofting it up into the overhead bin. It's because I'm challenged with being patient and I don't want to waste time waiting for luggage when I get to my destination. Most of all, I want control of my bag. Otherwise, there is no guarantee my luggage will arrive when I do.

The funny thing is, every now and then, I see folks get on the plane with a small bag, a book, and a cup of coffee. I marvel at that spectacle, gazing in awe and observing the freedom they have from all their excess baggage. Then I find myself thinking about what it would be like to release control of my luggage and walk through the airport carrying only what I need on the plane. A girl can dream...

Yet, this illustrates exactly what happens when we choose to break up with control as we know it: we travel through life more lightly, because we lose the excess baggage that comes with trying to control everything.

That doesn't mean we'll fly through our years on earth with clear skies. The ride will get bumpy and storms will come. Life will get complicated and unexplainable, and there'll be times when we don't feel like God is in control because we don't understand what's happening around us. But here's the deal: even when we don't *feel* like God is in control, He. Still. Is.

Friends, there is so much freedom from the busyness of control when we choose to travel more lightly. There is so much rest that awaits when we begin to view our circumstances through God's incredible love for us, instead of viewing God through our circumstances. The invitation to really let go and let God is lavish. And the more we mindfully practice letting God be God, the more we can experience his faithfulness at a new level.

Trust, rest, and begin to receive.

rest

---

*Do not worry. Learn to pray about
everything. Give thanks to God as
you ask him for what you need.
The peace of God is much greater
than the human mind can understand.
This peace will keep your hearts and
minds through Christ Jesus.*
Philippians 4:6 – 7 NLT

breaking up with control

- Breaking up with control as you know it takes courage. It requires you to loosen your white-knuckle grip on life as you think it *should* be. It requires you to live confidently as you pursue your dreams and goals while at the same time remaining humble and open to God's direction and detours.

- A control-addicted life is not a deliberate life based on God's truths. It's a stressful life often rooted in fear. Releasing your need to control what you can't control is a big step in letting God be God.

- Letting go of the need for control is an active part of your faith walk that requires deliberate decisions around your actions and behaviors. It's a process where you intentionally pursue an understanding of God's truth about your life instead of living by destructive fear-driven feelings.

- You need self-control to break up with control. God's idea of self-control is not legalistic or restrictive; it is the path to true and meaningful freedom.

- God is your ultimate provider. He loves you unconditionally and will provide for your needs. Standing on that truth can transform the busyness of control into a posture of surrender.

- God is in control, even when you don't feel like he is. Freedom and rest await when you begin to view your circumstances through God's incredible love for you, instead of viewing God through your circumstances.

ditch the
distracted mind

If destruction fails to entangle us,
distraction will do its best.
Beth Moore

The secret of the Christian life...
is that you don't have to figure it out.
You don't have to figure life out,
you don't have to figure each other out,
you don't have to figure parenting out,
or money or family.
You have a Counselor, you have a Guide,
you have God.
What a relief that we don't have
to figure it all out.
John Eldredge

Patience with others is Love.
Patience with self is Hope.
Patience with God, is FAITH.
Adel Bestavaros

You're only here for a short visit.
Don't hurry, don't worry.
And be sure to smell the flowers
along the way.
Walter Hagen

God did not create you to live a distracted life.
God created you to live a Jesus-infused life.
Margaret Feinberg

shoeless

CRAVE PRESENT-MOMENT LIVING

I've learned a lot on my path to living more deliberately, including that my own distracted mind provides plenty of material for our Chapter 4 conversation.

Case in point: There was a time early in the journey where I was mindfully (not!) gathering my things to leave the house for an appointment. As I grabbed my purse and headed toward the door, something didn't feel right. I looked down at my feet and quickly understood why: I had forgotten to put on my shoes. I wish I was kidding. A good friend pointed out that at least I was wearing socks, so I shouldn't feel *too* bad. (Thank you, Jesus, for encouraging friends!)

Welcome to my world.

I could fill an entire chapter with anecdotes like this. Most are less dramatic, like forgotten shopping lists, misplaced keys, or lost sunglasses. Yet, regardless of the drama-factor, I can safely say I have a lot of experience in forgetting things. Or forgetting where I've put things.

Ironically, I don't think it's because I'm inherently forgetful. Most of the time, it's because my mind is distracted from the present moment. I am on to the *next* thing at the expense of the *now* thing.

Sometimes, the distractions are visible. House or office clutter. Cell phone. Emails. Staring at my over-full calendar. Often, however, it's the invisible mental clutter that distracts me the most.

I am distracted by where I'm going.

I am distracted by where I've been.

I am distracted trying to figure out stuff.

I am distracted worrying about stuff.

I am distracted by the would haves. Could haves.
Should haves. And the dids.

Granted, it's not a big deal if we forget small stuff now and then. But it is a big deal when we allow our mental distractions to take up so much brain space that we lose touch with the present moment. In the broader scheme of the deliberate life, it also becomes a big deal when *we're more diverted by our distractions than we are devoted to trusting God.*

As a hard-wired doer and thinker, I know ditching my mental distractions doesn't come naturally. I also know the more I practice trading my distracted mind for a deliberate mind, the more I am learning to crave the gift that comes in present-moment living.

I don't care as much about forgetting my shoes as I care about missing my moments.

test it

─────────────────○─────────────────

When we crave something, like a favorite food, we usually find a way to satisfy it.

What does it look like for you to crave present-moment living? Identify your biggest challenges with both visible and invisible distractions. What doable steps can you take to limit those distractions in the scope of your daily routine?

my notes

_____

_____

_____

_____

_____

_____

_____

_____

_____

_____

_____

_____

trust it

Steep your life in God-reality. God-initiative. God provisions. Don't worry about missing out. You'll find out all of your everyday human concerns will be met. Give your entire attention to what God is doing right now, and don't get worked up about what may or may not happen tomorrow. God will help you deal with whatever hard things come up when the time comes.
Matthew 6:33 -34 The Message

monkey brain

Admittedly, I am not a telephone person. While I value hearing the voices of the people I love, most of my friends and family know where I stand on this phone thing.

So, when a friend called one night just before we sat down to dinner, it got my attention. She said she had news to share, but assured me the news wasn't urgent so we made plans to chat later on.

I was not comfortable with this uncertainty, especially since it was hanging over my head during mealtime. Naturally, my monkey brain got busy trying to figure out her news. Soon, instead of being completely present in the table conversation with Jay, I was distracted with my own mental conversation. I ran several scenarios in my mind. Given some of the recent communications with my friend, I was certain I had it pegged.

I wasn't even close.

What she shared with me was completely different from what I expected. We both laughed, because even she knew I would probably draw the wrong conclusion.

While this is a simple example, I believe it shows what happens when we're uncomfortable with uncertainty: we get distracted by "figuring out."

We figure out what to say in conversations that never occur.

We figure out solutions to problems we never have.

We figure out how we will respond when life throws us a curve ball that never ends up coming our way.

We figure out what people are saying behind our backs, when they aren't really saying anything at all.

No doubt, when we're consumed in *figuring out*, it's not long before we're consumed in *worrying about*. That, my friends, is another treadmill to nowhere.

Yes, we need to plan and prepare to steward our decisions well. Yes, we need to put on our big-kid pants and act to address the real situations that arise in our lives. But when we overdose on figuring out, we lose perspective. It's almost like we're putting more faith in ourselves to deal with life's issues instead of putting faith in God to take care of us when the real stuff happens.

Uncertainty is uncomfortable. But the Lord's unconditional love for us is the certainty we need to live less distracted and enjoy our life now.

test it

The distraction of figuring out is a surefire way to get ahead of God. The more we practice living in the mystery, the more we learn to cultivate greater trust in him.

Consider the four examples of figuring out from the previous page. Do any of these resonate with you? Or is there another type of figuring out that consumes your mind? Next time you catch yourself in that head space, use it as a prompt to stop and get in your heart space. Remind yourself that God is working it out for you. Then take a breath, let it go, and return to the present moment.

my notes

trust it

Trust God from the bottom of your heart;
don't try to figure out everything on your own.
Listen for God's voice in everything you do,
everywhere you go; he's the one who will keep
you on track. Don't assume that you know it all.
Run to God! Run from evil! Your body will glow
with health, your very bones will vibrate with life!
Proverbs 3:5 – 8 The Message

sometime around 4

―――――○―――――

LET GO OF THE "IF" FAMILY

Practicing the deliberate life has aided my health on a lot of levels, especially when it comes to improving my sleep habits. Aside from making better pre-bedtime choices, I've found that less is often more when it comes to resting well. Less worry, more sleep. Less figuring out, more sleep. Less striving for perfection, more sleep.

All that said, I still have times – usually around 4 in the morning – when I wake up and my mind gets busy. Sometimes, whether I like it or not, I do believe it's God waking me up to talk, because that's the only time he can get my full attention. But other times, it's these mental creatures I've not-so-affectionately named the "If" family: "If Only" and "What If."

Problem is, the If family not only show up in the wee hours of the morning to rob my sleep, they also show up during the day to distract my healthy thinking.

"If Only" likes to distract me with guilt and regret: "*If only* I had made a better decision about that situation. *If only* I had x-y-z then life would work better. *If only* I hadn't said x-y-z then I wouldn't feel so stupid."

On the other hand, "What If" likes to distract me by sowing seeds of fear and insecurity: "*What if* I make the wrong decision? *What if* they don't like me? *What if* I fail? *What if* I succeed? *What if* I'm not doing enough?"

I've seen in my own life, when I default to "If Only," the regret dweller in me begins focusing on my imperfect past instead of the perfect God who holds my future. When I default to "What If," the control freak in me arises and, before I know it, I'm spending more time in that exhausting pattern of worrying about what's next instead of praying about it and letting it go.

The distractions of "If Only" and "What If" each have unique ways of sneaking into our brains, but they are united when it comes to their purpose: to steal our peace. To steal our joy. To steal our present moments.

My conclusion: living less distracted happens when we kick the If family to the curb. It happens when we mindfully turn our thoughts to the hope of the Gospel: Jesus died on the cross so both our past and future are covered...and we get grace for today.

Choosing to stand on the truth, one "If" at a time, is a deliberate path to greater peace.

test it

"What If" and "If Only" not only steal our present moments, they steal our contentment and our joy.

Which "If" is your biggest challenge: "What if" or "If Only"? What part of that can you be mindful to turn over to God? Take the scriptures on the next page, write them down, or put them in your phone and make sure they're easily found. Next time the If family shows up, pull out these scriptures and be reminded God has your back <u>and</u> your future.

my notes

_____

_____

_____

_____

_____

_____

_____

_____

_____

_____

trust it

―――――――――――――――――◇―――――――――――――――――

*"Forget the former things; do not dwell
on the past. See, I am doing a new thing!
Now it springs up; do you not perceive it?
I am making a way in the
desert and streams in the wasteland."*
Isaiah 43:18 – 19

*"For I know the plans I have for you,"
declares the LORD, "plans to prosper
you and not to harm you, plans to give
you hope and a future."*
Jeremiah 29:11

the greener grass

BEWARE OF UNHEALTHY UNHAPPINESS

I spent many years being unhappy in my job assignments. Sometimes, even though I was busy, I was bored. Other times, the busyness is what fed my discontent. I had a habit of convincing myself the grass would be greener *if only* I could have a job on the other side of the fence—perhaps doing something I was passionate about.

Because I enjoy all things wellness and fitness, I once became certified as a personal trainer—even as I was ghost-writing a substantial book, among other client projects. Another time, because I'm a tad bit obsessive about travel, I decided that being a part-time travel agent would make me happy. And I wish those were the only two examples.

My client work never suffered from these distractions. But I did.

Thankfully, I'm a lot wiser these days. While I know not everyone can relate to my job distractions, I believe we can all relate to the power of unhealthy unhappiness and how it can manifest. In our jobs. Parenting roles. Relationships. Acquisition of material things. You name it.

How do we know when we have unhealthy unhappiness?

Here's what I've experienced: When an unhealthy unhappiness seeps into some area of my life, my peace with who I am, where I am, and what I have seeps out. When peace exits, trouble begins. My thinking gets distracted and, when that happens, my life is not too far behind.

To be clear, I'm not advocating we stay in bad situations or get complacent in pursuing our passions. I believe the Lord will stir healthy discontent—that's what draws our awareness to making wrong things right and incents us to create positive change in our lives and in the world.

What I'm talking about is the kind of unhappiness that draws our mind into the *scarcity of what is not,* instead of the *appreciation for what is.* The kind that distracts us from the opportunities we have at our fingertips to bloom and bless others where we're planted. In our current season. In the current assignment. In the day. In the hour. In the moment.

I know God has redeemed my job adventures and worked them all for good as part of my story. I also grieve when I think about the cost of those distractions—the time, energy, and money I spent trying to achieve that better thing I thought would make me happy. I don't have it all figured out, of course. But I have learned that having a more deliberate mind means I stop giving unhealthy unhappiness such power in my life.

Cultivating a lasting joy in the Lord is always better than striving for fleeting happiness.

test it

———————————○———————————

Unhealthy unhappiness can have power in our lives to the point where it drives us to distracted, unfocused living.

Think about an area of your life where it has had too much power. How did it show up in your decision-making? Was there a cost? How did it make your life more complex? Next time you sense some unhealthy unhappiness surfacing, redirect your mind to avoid the distraction. Think about how you can bloom today, where you are, and with the people around you. Getting our mind on others is a great way to get it off our unhappiness.

my notes

_____

_____

_____

_____

_____

_____

_____

_____

trust it

───────────○───────────

Keep your eyes straight ahead; ignore all sideshow distractions. Watch your step, and the road will stretch out smooth before you. Look neither right nor left; leave evil in the dust.
Proverbs 4:26 – 27 The Message

safe travels

LEARN TO WAIT WELL

Jay and I had a goal to visit all fifty states before each of us turned fifty years old. I'm humbly grateful we've attained that goal—part by intention, part by business travel, and part by family vacations growing up.

Jay's fiftieth state was Oregon, so we made it a vacation to celebrate. It was supposed to be a simple trip—St. Louis to Denver, then on to Portland, Oregon. Afternoon arrival, in time for dinner.

As it turns out, it wasn't so simple. Due to thunderstorms in Denver, our flight was re-routed to Oklahoma City, where we waited on the tarmac. Then we went on to Denver, where we waited some more. Next was Reno, where we changed planes and waited again. Finally, at midnight, we arrived in Portland. It was a long day of hurry-up-and-wait, to say the least. This wasn't our plan for the journey. However, we chose to be patient and enjoy the adventure, knowing the decision to re-route our plane was done for our own protection.

I wish I could say I have exercised that much patience when it comes to waiting on God.

Thing is, in this case, the airline did a great job keeping us informed as to what was happening, why we were waiting, and where we were going next.

Traveling with God isn't always that transparent.

We have plans and a destination in mind, but life happens. Things get delayed. We try and figure out why our plans aren't working. We blame ourselves for not being good enough to make them work, or we blame God for not listening. In our impatience, however, we usually don't slow down. We often speed up. We make new plans we think will work. Followed by a to-do list of actions that will accelerate our journey to the ideal place at our ideal time.

Brothers and sisters, managing our plans is not a bad thing. But when our plans and impatience begin to manage us, that's when the distraction begins. That's when we start missing out on the peace that comes from fully trusting God's timing *and* protection.

Learning to wait well is hard. It requires us to mindfully stop. Maybe even lay down our plans for a short season, so we can get out of our own way and create some space for God to reveal a better plan. The Lord's itinerary may look different and the destination may even be different. But thankfully, unlike the airlines, God is always punctual. He is never late *and* he is also never early.

Impatience can open the door to distraction, but waiting well is a luxurious invitation into the present moment. It is an expansive invitation that allows us to practice a greater trust in God for his timing, not ours.

test it

Impatience tempts us to forge ahead with our plans and then ask God to bless them, instead of laying our plans in front of God, asking for his guidance, and choosing to wait well.

When has your impatience opened the door to distractions? How could you have practiced waiting well in that situation? Learning to wait well takes practice, so give it a shot in your everyday present moments. Take a deep breath next time you're in the slow line at the grocery store. Or when your technology doesn't cooperate. Or in traffic when you're running late to a meeting. Be appreciative of where you are in that moment. Find something positive in the landscape around you, and thank God for it.

my notes

trust it

─────────────○─────────────

Wait on the Lord; Be of good courage,
And he shall strengthen your heart;
Wait, I say, on the Lord!
Psalm 27:14 NKJV

enjoying the gift

———————◦———————

STOP DOING LIFE AS A FLY-BY

While I don't consider myself a "flowers and candy" gal, I'll admit Jay can't go wrong when he brings me roses and dark chocolate. I'm a woman, after all. Some things just go with the territory.

I remember one birthday when he surprised me with a dozen roses. After finding a perfect vase, I strategically placed the enormous bouquet on our kitchen island—a convenient place for watering and a major traffic area where I could frequently see and enjoy the gift.

During this particular week, however, I was in the middle of an intense client project. To that end, a couple days after my birthday, I went to the kitchen to grab some water and take a much-needed mental break from my home office. On the way to the sink, I noticed the roses and began to miss Jay, who was traveling for work. In that momentary space of loneliness, something shifted in my busy brain. Instead of flying by the island to quickly fill my glass, I chose to stop and look at the roses—*really* look at them. When I did, I immediately saw how much they needed water. Despite my strategic placement near the faucet, I had not once filled the vase, which was par for the course in my chronically-hurried world.

Mostly, however, I noticed how the flowers had opened to full bloom and had become even more beautiful than the day I received them. I know it's going to sound cliché, but I not only stopped—I smelled the roses. It was in the simplicity of stopping and looking and smelling that I found myself truly enjoying the gift.

I remember this moment like it was yesterday, to the point where I feel tears as I write. Those roses were more than a present. They represented a precious expression of Jay's heart, something I didn't fully appreciate because I was distracted by my work and also by everything else around me in the kitchen—the newspaper on the table, the dishes in the sink, the unopened mail on the counter. I realized I was more captivated by my chaos than I was by the expression of my husband's love. Talk about a wakeup call.

Friends, this journey to ditch our distracted mind won't happen overnight. If you're wired like me, it won't fully happen this side of heaven—especially given the world of amped-up technology we live in today. But remember, our progress is more important than our perfect.

My big, hairy audacious prayer for the *deliberate* Tribe is that we learn to crave present-moment living. I pray that through our craving we become an example of living less distracted. I pray we are the ones who choose to put away our electronic distractions when we're with others. I pray we are the ones who get a grip on our mental distractions so we can share the peace that comes from waiting well. I pray we, by our actions,inspire others to stop doing life as a fly-by. To breathe, rest, and simply be.

rest

It is not good to be a person without knowledge.
He who hurries often misses the way.
Proverbs 19:2 NSV

ditch the distracted mind

- Ditching your mental distractions doesn't come naturally. The more you practice trading your distracted mind for a deliberate mind, the more you can learn to crave the gift that comes in present-moment living.

- When you're uncomfortable with uncertainty, make a deliberate choice to do less figuring out and more praying about.

- The distractions of "If Only" and "What If" can steal your peace, your joy, and your present moments. Choosing to stand on the truth, one "If" at a time, is a deliberate path to peace.

- Unhealthy unhappiness distracts your mind to focus on scarcity and what you don't have. Learn to appreciate where you are, in your current season and assignment. Look for opportunities to bloom and bless others where you're planted.

- God is always punctual. Waiting well is an expansive invitation that allows you to practice trusting God on a greater level.

- Your progress is more important than your perfect. You can trade your distracted mind for a deliberate mind by moving the needle a little bit each day, using each mental distraction as an opportunity to stop, breathe, refocus, and pray. Even the smallest prayer can redirect your mind to the goodness of God and away from the over-consuming commotion of life.

get serious
about breathing room

We have value beyond what we produce and achieve.
In fact, we are accepted by God before we do
or achieve anything important.
Don Postema

The decisions you make determine the schedule
you keep. The schedule you keep determines the
life you live. And how you live your life determines
how you spend your soul.
Lysa Terkeurst

In the rush and noise of life, as you have intervals,
step home within yourselves and be still.
Wait upon God, and feel his good presence; this
will carry you evenly through your day's business.
William Penn

Our busyness keeps us fluttering like a pollinating bee
that hardly stops long enough for a sip of nectar. There
are worlds inside each of us that remain unseen until
we step in close and stare. It's an intentional stopping.
Don't kid yourself into thinking a glance is the same
thing as a stare. A sip is not a gulp.
Elizabeth Koziatek

The quieter you become, the more you can hear.
Ram Dass

dangerous intersections

———————————◦———————————

HEED THE STOP SIGNS

We live in a great neighborhood with beautiful mature trees and green space bordering the subdivision. It's not a bad scene for old-school suburbia and it has enough nature to make for enjoyable walks. We don't, however, have many sidewalks. So, naturally, we're extra careful at the four-way intersections because most drivers ignore the stop signs. Of course, they need to be looking up from their smart phones to *see* the signs... but alas, I digress.

Anyway, I remember one day when I took a break from writing to walk our dog. It was the middle of the afternoon and traffic was light. Even so, I took my usual extended cautionary pause at the four-way intersections. It was then I witnessed a modern day miracle.

I saw two drivers who chose to fully stop. No fly-by. No slow roll. They actually *stopped*.

It's sad this is the exception more than the rule, hence a "modern day miracle." Scary thing is, I think we can find ourselves driving through life the same way we drive our cars.

We live dangerously overwhelmed because we consider the act of stopping to be optional.

For whatever reason, we think we can't stop because of everything that "needs" to get done. Or we don't stop because, subconsciously, we are getting our identity and defining our value through activity. Or we won't stop because we fear the potentially uncomfortable space of silence in our lives.

Problem is, over time, a perpetual pattern of go-go-go can impact us on all levels. It can show up mentally when we become scattered, impatient, unfocused, anxious, or quick to anger. It can manifest in the physical body through over-exertion, injury, sleeplessness, illness, or unhealthy eating habits. It can even shut us down spiritually when we get so consumed in our doing we don't make time for being. All these manifestations are stop signs that beg for our attention. Yet, we keep going. Instead of living a rested life with more breathing room, we live an *arrested* life imprisoned by patterns of chronic activity.

Friends, heed the stop signs. Change your perspective and get some breathing room in your life. It's time to thrive, not just survive!

test it

———————————○———————————

Choosing to stop is foundational in the practice of creating more breathing room in our lives.

Are you experiencing any of the mental, physical, or spiritual stop signs mentioned in the lesson—or perhaps another stop sign—that you continue to ignore? If the pattern continues, what will be the cost? This week when you're out driving your car, be intentional to stop at the stop signs and drive the speed limit. The awareness gained from these basic (and lawful) activities can be eye-opening and, in turn, provide a reminder on the importance of heeding the mental, physical, and spiritual stop signs in your life.

my notes

_____

_____

_____

_____

_____

_____

_____

_____

trust it

─────────○─────────

Step out of the traffic! Take a long,
loving look at me, your High God.
Psalm 46:10 The Message

a case for space (and punctuation)

I've been a writer in some capacity for most of my time on earth. I wrote fiction stories for fun as a young child. I became editor of the high school yearbook in my teens. Eventually, I became a professional corporate communicator writing speeches, video scripts, and just about anything in business communications that required content and messaging. Funny thing is, when I tell people about my tapestry, they often assume that I liked English class or was an English major. That's not the case. In fact, I find many of the rules and regulations about "proper" English to be a bit restrictive when it comes to writing clearly. Easy reading is hard writing. Sometimes, I need to break the rules to be understood and relevant to how we speak in everyday conversation.

That said, there are two obvious rules of good writing that can't be broken...and you don't have to be a writer to know them:

1) Leave space between words.

2) Use punctuation.

Can you imagine what it would be like to read a paragraph if we didn't operate in those boundaries?

Itwouldlooksomethinglikethisonesentenceafteranotherwordafter wordparagraphafterparagraphjusthowmuchofthatcouldyoutake beforeyourheadsstartsspinningandyoustopreadingnotmuch.

You get the picture.

How does this translate into breathing room, you ask? As human *doings*, it seems as if it's become habitual (and almost applauded) to live our lives without boundaries and plow through our days as one big run-on sentence. In our constant cycle of busyness, we not only blow past the stop signs, we completely miss the importance and value of space in our lives.

Space for self-care.

Space for soul care.

Space to simply breathe.

Whether it's professionally, personally and/or socially, I'm not sure what exactly propels us into the boundary-less habit of chronic doing. It's probably a combination of things. For some, I think it's stuff we've already talked about—behavior patterns such as perfection, control, people-pleasing, and fear of missing out. For others, it might be an underlying feeling that breathing room must be *earned* and we aren't worthy of downtime if we haven't done enough to deserve it.

Whatever the case, run-on sentence living is no way to live. When it comes to practicing the deliberate life, being intentional to set boundaries and opt out of chronic doing will ultimately strengthen us for every part of our journey. Mind, body, and soul.

test it

———————————○———————————

Chronic doing exists when we find ourselves in a cycle of constant activity without boundaries to guard our breathing room.

Which aspect of chronic doing (professional, personal, social) is your biggest challenge? What drives it? Where can you push the "pause" button this week, even on a good thing, to create a little more breathing room?

my notes

trust it

The Spirit of God has made me;
the breath of the Almighty gives me life.
Job 33:4

the unhurried life

When I traveled frequently for my consulting business, I became fond of airport shopping. Seriously, why waste time sitting in the gate area to wait for the plane? I needed to be doing something. And to be honest, a little retail therapy after a long week of client meetings felt pretty awesome.

I especially liked the book stores. I found it gratifying and ultimately relaxing to find a new book, get on the plane, and enjoy downtime up at 30,000 feet with laptop off and soul-food reading in hand.

One author I discovered in my airport travels was John Ortberg. I was permanently marked by a story he shared about a conversation with his mentor Dallas Willard, a professor of philosophy and Christian author.

In a nutshell, John had asked Dallas what he needed to do to be spiritually healthy. Dallas' response: "You must ruthlessly eliminate hurry from your life."[4]

When John pressed him for something more, Dallas stood firm. "There is nothing else," he said. "You must ruthlessly eliminate hurry from your life."

Oh, is *that* all?

At the time, I lived in a perpetual state of hurry. Sometimes, it was an over-achieving hurry, convincing myself I could "get it all done" and "do one more thing" before I left the office or house for an appointment. Other times, it was an over-committed hurry, resulting from an over-full calendar. In some cases, it was an attitude of hurry. I was too impatient to embrace the space in life so I felt the need to do something. Doing fed my hurry and hurry kept me doing. It was a constant spiral.

I don't know if you can relate to any aspect of this, but I'm guessing most of us experience the spiral of doing and hurrying at various points in our life journey. Even if it is not sustained over many years, it is a concern when it happens. The spiral is not only dangerous to our physical selves, it robs our peace, our joy, and diverts us from the deliberate path. Worse yet, I believe hurry can be an enemy to growing in our faith. We hurry and read our devotionals. We hurry up and get to church. And then we hurry on to living the rest of our lives. In a hurry.

Ortberg points out:

For most of us, the great danger [of hurry] is not that we will renounce our faith. It is that we will become so distracted and rushed and preoccupied that we will settle for a mediocre version of it. We will just skim our lives instead of actually living them.[5]

Yikes! I don't know about you, but the thought of skimming my life is downright scary. Life is precious. Time is precious. Why would we choose a hurried life of skimming when we can choose an unhurried life of truly living?

test it

Whether we recognize it or not, our choices often drive our hurry.

Next time you find yourself in the spiral of doing and hurry, be intentional to stop, breathe, and ask yourself: What is at the root of my rush? Over-achievement, over-commitment, or impatience? Something else? What small and immediate shift can you make in your schedule or behavior to create more breathing room between your commitments and tasks?

my notes

trust it

―――――――――――――――○―――――――――――――――

Slow down. Take a deep breath.
What's the hurry? Why wear yourself out?
Just what are you after anyway? But you say,
"I can't help it. I'm addicted to alien gods.
I can't quit."
Jeremiah 2:25 The Message

mindful running

TRADE TRYING FOR TRAINING

My greatest inspiration for writing these lessons usually comes when I'm not sitting at the computer.

I remember when it came in the dental chair during a conversation with my dentist. I say "conversation" loosely. As you know, there's not much two-way chatting that happens when you're the one in the chair. Which is fine, because it takes my mind off my mouth.

On this visit, my dentist—an avid runner—shared a discussion he had with a friend regarding the strategy to running faster. In my best dental chair mumble, I asked, "What's the secret?"

According to his running buddy, the secret wasn't rocket science. The way to run faster? You train. Then you run faster.

Simple, yet profound. Serious runners don't just try to run faster. They mindfully train their bodies and they learn to run faster.

I understand the irony here. This chapter is about breathing room and rest. Yet, the punch line implies, "Get up and do it." What gives?

The point is this: If we want to create breathing room in life, we can't just try to make changes. Think about it. We can try to slow down. We can try to take better care of ourselves. We can try to spend more time with God. But here's the deal: either we do it or we don't—that's where the rubber meets the road. Even when our intentions are strong, I believe "try" is a fairly weak word often followed by a series of excuses as to why we're not making progress. It's like running a race without even leaving the starting block—we end up going nowhere.

Friends, let's trade trying for training! Let's stop making excuses and turn intention into reality by scheduling time for breathing room—just like we schedule (and re-schedule) any other priority in life.

I realize this lesson is more tactical than most in the *deliberate* book, yet with good reason. In my experience teaching the *deliberate* concepts, I've seen a great awakening in tired spirits when people own the idea that soul care and self-care are not selfish. We cannot live, let alone give, out of an empty tank. On any level.

There is only one you. The world needs you. And you are worth the breathing room.

test it

———————————◦———————————

When we trade trying for training, we are taking intentional action to let go of clutter in our schedules to create space in our lives.

What do soul care and self-care look like to you? Where do you find yourself "trying" to do these things, but not making any progress? Without becoming overly legalistic or perfectionistic, be intentional to plan some soul care and self-care this week. Then keep up the practice in the weeks ahead. Start small if necessary. The point is to schedule breathing room on your calendar just like you would anything else important in your life. If you need to re-book it as things happen, no problem. Just don't cancel it.

my notes

_____

_____

_____

_____

_____

_____

_____

trust it

─────────────○─────────────

We are merely moving shadows, and all our
busy rushing ends in nothing.
Psalm 39:6 NLT

the white flag

FLEX YOUR SURRENDER MUSCLES

I enjoyed several things about the self-publishing process. I got to work with an incredible mentor and friend. I had input into my deadlines and freedom to adjust when necessary. I also got to gather the very first *deliberate* Tribe—the group of amazing folks who graciously gave their time as beta readers and reviewed the first manuscript.

On the other hand, what I didn't enjoy about the process was when God tested me on the very things I wrote about. This chapter was no exception. I had my idea of the theme. I had my idea of lessons it would include. I had my idea of when I wanted it finished. But I struggled. Nothing came together according to plan. The struggle got so intense I had to heed the stop signs and consider opting out of my chronic doing.

Go figure.

As I laid in bed one morning knowing I would miss a deadline to the beta readers, I felt defeated and weak. I thought, "This is what you get, Kathy, for writing about surrender. Now *you* must surrender. To the writer's block. To your expectations.

To the things in your life beyond your control that are getting in the way." In my half-awake state, I uttered helplessly, "I surrender, God."

At that moment, God met me in my weak prayer and something shifted. I saw clearly that I was the only one forcing the deadline. I was the only one in the way of my breathing room. I realized in focusing so much on my ideal plan for the book, I got sucked into forced doing and had created my own prison within the process. Bam. I tasted freedom.

Within a few minutes of the revelation, I jumped out of bed to write a transparent (and therapeutic) email to the tribe explaining the situation. Before hitting "send," I went to get a cup of tea. While waiting for the water to boil, a mental light went on and I had a major epiphany about this chapter. I couldn't stop my brain from flowing. I sent the email and then stayed at the keyboard to work on the book, accomplishing more in four hours than in the previous four weeks.

I can't tell you exactly what shifted in my mind that morning. I thought I had already surrendered. I thought I was giving God control. Yet, the Lord knew differently. I believe he needed me to grow through the struggle and was patiently waiting for me to get on my heart-knees in a place of raw weakness. A place where I truly surrendered my expectations for his faithfulness.

I wish I could say my struggle with surrender is finished. I wish I could say surrender is something I schedule on my calendar like I do self-care. Yet, I can't say that and look you in the eye. I can, however, testify: the more I exercise the discipline to flex my surrender muscles, the more freedom I experience from my chronic doing and the more I find breathing room in my life.

In God's way of doing things, waving the white flag of surrender does not make us prisoners of an enemy. It allows us to be captured and captivated by an amazing God who is proven faithful and whose love never fails—and *that* is the ultimate place to breathe.

test it

The best way to flex our surrender muscles is to train them with exercise.

Think about your task list and/or your active work or home projects. Which ones are self-imposed deadlines? Of those, which one is causing you the most anxiety? Now go ahead and lay it down. Walk away. For a week, a month—however long you feel led. When the time is over, return to the task/project. You may find a fresh perspective and new energy. You may have clarity on a better plan to move forward with ease. Or you may even find the task or project is no longer as important as you thought. Be open and aware to what God shows you in your breathing room.

my notes

_____

_____

_____

_____

_____

_____

_____

trust it

But he said to me, "My grace is sufficient for you, for my power is made perfect in weakness." Therefore, I will boast all the more gladly about my weaknesses, so that Christ's power may rest on me.
2 Corinthians 12:9

checking out

EXPERIENCE THE VALUE OF SILENCE

Before I launched into writing this book, I completed a substantial client assignment that consumed most of my waking hours. We were sharing information globally in different time zones and the pace of change required me to stay connected with email in real-time. My smart phone was practically glued to my fingertips.

This specific engagement came in a season of life where the constant phone attachment was no longer the norm for me. I had already become intentional to take a Sabbath from my electronics. Yet, I knew the project had a finite ending and the intensity would be relatively short-term. With that in mind, I said yes, did the work, and—by the grace of God—found peace, even in the chaos.

Once the assignment concluded, I noticed something I hadn't heard in a while: silence. The endless email strings had subsided. The chatter stopped. I had freedom from the noise.

Ironically, however, I ignored that freedom. I found myself habitually checking my cell phone for emails and texts. Wow—I was amazed at how subtly this plugged-in behavior crept back into my life. In only a few short weeks, I was transformed from a mindful woman who chose silence to a mindless woman who checked her phone because it was there. Yet, I'm not alone. One report says the average person checks their phone 110 times per day, while the more addicted check their phones as much as 900 times per day.[6] Wow!

I was humbled as I reflected on the power of that re-surfacing habit. I was also reminded how challenging it is to choose silence in our amped-up world. We not only have noise from our electronics and social media, we have the noise of our to-do lists. We have the noise of our schedules. We have noise from the people in our lives.

Obviously, the noise in and of itself is not a bad thing. Where we cross the line is when we allow the noise to suffocate our breathing room.

In the book *Sacred Rhythms,* author Ruth Barton sums it up nicely:

Constant noise, interruption and drivenness to be more productive cut us off from—or at least interrupts—the direct experience of God and other human beings. This is more isolating than we recognize. Because we are experiencing less meaningful human and divine connection, we are emptier relationally, and we try harder and harder to fill that loneliness with even more noise and stimulation. In so doing, we lose touch with the quieter and more subtle experiences of God within.[7]

This is a vicious cycle indeed.

Solitude is an opportunity to interrupt this cycle by turning off the noise and stimulation of our lives so that we can hear our loneliness and our longing calling us deeper into the only relationship that can satisfy our longing.

Choosing to have moments of silence and solitude is a small step away from chronic doing and a big step toward knowing God and knowing yourself on a deeper level. Instead of checking in, check out! Lose the noise, exhale, and discover the restoration that waits for you in the quiet.

rest

The Lord will fight for you,
and you have only to be silent.
Exodus 14:14 ESV

get serious about breathing room

- The deliberate life is a *rested* life with more breathing room, rather than an *arrested* life imprisoned by patterns of chronic activity.

- Setting boundaries and opting out of chronic doing will ultimately strengthen you for every part of the journey— mind, body, and soul.

- Hurry is a thief. It robs your peace, your joy, and your present moments. It can also be an enemy to growing in your faith.

- Soul care and self-care are not selfish. You cannot live, let alone give, out of an empty tank. You are worth the breathing room.

- In God's way of doing things, waving the white flag of surrender does not make you a prisoner of an enemy. It allows you to be captured and captivated by an amazing God who is proven faithful and whose love never fails— that is the ultimate place to breathe.

- Choosing to have moments of silence and solitude is a small step away from chronic doing and a big step toward knowing God and knowing yourself on a deeper level. There is restoration waiting for you in the quiet.

grow deeper with God

*Never try to have more faith...just get to know
God better. And because God is faithful,
the better you know him the more you'll trust him.*
John Ortberg

*There is a freedom that comes from being
who we are in God and resting in God
that eventually enables us to bring something
truer to the world than all our doing.*
Ruth Barton

*Imagine for a moment the limitlessness of being
identified not by what we do, but by Whose we are.
You are his chosen, beloved, righteous, wanted, holy,
valuable, equipped, essential, radiant and wise [child]...
all because of what Jesus did for you. Nothing you
could ever do can upstage that, so we are free to
stop trying and just be with God because of Jesus.*
Stephanie Haynes

*If prayer is the expression of the human heart in
conversation with God, it is also the expression of
God's heart to us. As we become more aware of
God's presence and activity in our lives, we begin to
recognize the ways he communicates with us.*
prayerventures.org

*Accomplishing the impossible is
about seeing the invisible.*
Steven Furtick

blender blowout

COME AS YOU ARE

Jay and I agree that enjoying healthy, well-prepared food is one of life's pleasures. However, we don't always agree about what *kind* of food we want to eat. He prefers meat to be the star player, whereas I am content with a plate full of veggies. That said, Jay does grill a mean slice of tofu and will even cook a meatless dinner for me on special occasions.

I remember one birthday when he planned an Indian-themed menu complete with soup, entrée, and dessert. Given my birthday girl status, I was relaxing on the patio with a book while Jay did his magic in the kitchen. But when I glanced through the kitchen window, my relaxation took a turn. I didn't see any magic. I only saw mess. Jay was pureeing soup in the blender and the lid exploded. Liquid went flying everywhere. The walls. The floors. The stove. The refrigerator. The cabinets. Just about anything in a five-foot radius was slimed with soup. I quickly traded my book for a rag and we began cleaning up the mess. Thankfully, not all the soup escaped and, despite the explosion, we got to enjoy a small and very delicious bowl.

As you know by now, I'm always looking for deeper lessons in my simpler life experiences. Upon reflection, I soon understood the message in the mess: there are days when I'm just like that soup–all over the place.

Despite my best-laid plans to keep things contained and in order, I get distracted. I get wrapped up in my own hurry. My brain gets messy. My decisions get messy. My actions get messy. On those days, the only thing that feels deliberate about my life is my decision to go to bed at night, and I even mess that up sometimes by staying up too late.

But here's the good news: even if we *feel* like that soup, God doesn't see us that way. Better yet, he doesn't ask us to get all cleaned up to grow deeper in our relationship with him. After all, he's God. He already knows our messes and he loves us anyway.

test it

———————————○———————————

God is always in control, even on the days when life feels all over the place.

Do you ever have days when you feel like that blender blowout? How do you typically react in those moments? How can you practice shifting your focus away from the mess and on to God? Today, be intentional to look for a message in any mess that comes your way. What might God be teaching you out of his love for you?

my notes

_____

_____

_____

_____

_____

_____

_____

_____

_____

_____

trust it

—o—

Even before he made the world, God loved us and chose us in Christ to be holy and without fault in his eyes. God decided in advance to adopt us into his own family by bringing us to himself through Jesus Christ. This is what he wanted to do, and it gave him great pleasure.

Ephesians 1:4 – 5 NLT

identity crisis

—————————————○—————————————

KNOW WHOSE YOU ARE

If you and I ever meet in person, I have one favor to ask. Please do *not* ask me, "What do you do?"

For some people, answering that question is like chatting about the weather—it's small talk. For me, however, I have despised that question—especially over the past twenty years. It was easy to answer early in my career when I had a job title or when I initially became self-employed as a "freelance writer." But as my consulting business progressed into more complex assignments, I found it increasingly difficult to answer succinctly, let alone in a way that would help people really understand my occupation. Most of the time, I'd get a head nod and a "Wow, that sounds interesting." I'm pretty sure it didn't.

I am even more frustrated by this question in my current season of life, as I'm navigating between what I've done for my job in the past to what my "work" will look like in the future. Because of that, and to make a very long story short, what I do changes almost every day and sometimes every hour. What's more, I'm not a parent and I'm still working, which means I don't even have the titles of "mom" or "retired" on my list of realistic options.

All that said, in my human desire to be understood, I have struggled with what I've often called an identity crisis. I realize that might sound overly dramatic. But let's face it: we live in a world where our identity—by default—is defined by our "labels." Labels wrapped up in our jobs, marital status, education, parenthood, friendships, hobbies, homes, automobiles, and the vacations we take (or don't take): "I am this... I do that... I have that..."

Friends, while our this-and-that has a place in our tapestry, it cannot be the source of our identity. If there's one thing I've learned in my own identity crisis, it's that my label as a *beloved child of God* is the only one that remains unchanged through my shifting seasons. No amount of life transition can take that away.

My mentor and fellow author Stephanie Haynes summed it up beautifully in one of her newsletters:

Adopting our identity as anything other than who God says we are leads to chaos in our lives. We all have been given gifts and talents to accomplish our part in God's grand tapestry for this world, but that is not who we are. In fact, it limits who we are; we are so much more than what we do![8]

Wow! It is so freeing to grasp that we are way more than what we do. Life's labels limit us, but God's love is limitless!

Remember: your identity is not just who you are, it's *whose* you are. A beloved child of God.

test it

Being purposeful to learn about and understand who we are in God's eyes is the best way to avoid an identity crisis in shifting seasons.

What labels do you use to define what you do? What's the risk of holding your identity in a label or job title? Make a list of five great qualities that describe who you are, not what you do. (Yes, you can find five!) Ask God to help you focus on those qualities as part of your identity through his eyes. Life is more about your "who" than your "do."

my notes

_____

_____

_____

_____

_____

_____

_____

_____

_____

_____

_____

_____

trust it

―――――――――○―――――――――

*See what great love the Father has
lavished on us, that we should be called
children of God! And that is what we are!*
1 John 3:1

life in the fast lane

Each year, our church encourages a three-week fasting period during the month of January. One of those weeks we fast an aspect of media or social media. During another we fast our mouths by releasing unhealthy conversation patterns. And, of course, there's one week when we fast food—either completely, or by giving up certain foods we enjoy eating. What I love about this yearly exercise is that we don't do it out of legalistic motivation. Rather we do it from a willingness to let go of permissible things so we can create space and ideally experience our need for God on a deeper level.

I remember one year during the food fast when I set aside 48 hours to consume only fruits and vegetables via juice or broth. Naturally, I learned a few things during this time, not the least of which is how much I enjoy chewing food instead of just drinking it. But most importantly, I learned how much I can miss chewing on God's Word.

You see, when I first decided to do the fast, I planned to combine fasting with longer, intentional periods of prayer and

Bible study. Easier said than done. As it turned out, I had an urgent and unexpected client project during those two days. Yes, I stuck to my 48-hour fast plan. However, as things turned out, I was basically starving myself out of obligation and my prayers were aimed at surviving the deadlines with my sanity intact. I noticed my stomach felt empty, but so did my heart. It was then I became less concerned about the hunger in my belly and more aware of the hunger in my soul.

Because the Lord is good all the time, including my crazy times, he gives grace abundantly, whether I ask for it or not. So even though I was off track in my intentions with the fast, God never was. He used even the small moments I spent praying for sanity to give me the gift of peace. Through it all, I was reminded God doesn't really measure his love for me by the length of my prayers. There is no prayer brief enough to offend God or long enough to impress God. While I fall short, he never does.

That said, when it comes to growing deeper with God, his love and grace are not an excuse to leave our faith and prayer life malnourished. Being intentional to know the Lord on a deeper level is not only the foundation for restoration, it's at the heart of our pursuit of living more deliberately.

test it

Just like food sustains our bodies, spiritual nourishment sustains our hearts and souls.

What would it look like in your world to more intentionally feed your faith? It needs to be doable, so get practical. Listen to worship songs while driving. Find a Bible-based podcast. Get up five minutes earlier for quiet time. Buy a new devotional book. We are all different. Just pick something and practice as soon as possible. Don't feel guilty about what you haven't done in the past. God is not a God of guilt. Every day is a new day with the Lord, and a new opportunity to get some nourishment for your soul.

my notes

_____

_____

_____

_____

_____

_____

_____

_____

trust it

─────────○─────────

Taste and see that the Lord is good;
Blessed is the man who trusts in him.
Psalm 34:8 NKJV

tomayto, tomahto

GET YOUR HOPES UP

In reviewing my journal writings from the past few years, I ran across an incident that reminded me of God's faithfulness. It's a story about tomatoes.

One summer Sunday while at the farmer's market, I received a text from a friend who invited me to stop by her house and pick up some home-grown tomatoes. Naturally, I didn't bother buying them at the market because I knew my friend's yummy tomatoes were coming. But when we stopped on the way home that day, she wasn't there. At the time, I didn't know her well enough to help myself. So alas, I returned home tomato-less.

Of course, this is not a serious issue by any means—I get that. But I did find myself at the kitchen counter that night hoping aloud, "Boy, God, I would just love to have a fresh tomato for my salad."

About five minutes after I verbalized my tomato crave, the doorbell rang. There stood the teenage girl from next door holding a big, beautiful tomato in her hand. She said, "We remembered you enjoy eating vegetarian and thought you might like this tomato." Obviously, I had to laugh at the timing of her visit. Then, I had to marvel at the expression of God's faithfulness to me in that simple utterance of hope.

The irony here is when it comes to the bigger things in life, I don't always speak hope-filled language. I catch myself saying, "Well, I'm excited about that, but I don't want to get my hopes up." I think, like most people, I use that phrase as a form of self-protection. After all, by not getting my hopes up, I don't have to be disappointed or look foolish in front of others if what I'm hoping for doesn't manifest.

But here's the deal: when we're doing life with God we can get our hopes up, because *God himself is hope.* Tribe, whether it's the big tomaytoes in life, or the small tomahtoes, let's hope expectantly and keep the faith!

test it

Viewing God himself as hope is an invitation to go deeper and grow our trust in him.

How willing are you to get your hopes up? What's the risk? What's the reward? Be intentional to get your hopes up today. Pray about one thing you're believing for and trust that God is working on your behalf.

my notes

_____

_____

_____

_____

_____

_____

_____

_____

_____

_____

_____

trust it

—————————————○—————————————

*Oh! May the God of green hope fill you up
with joy, fill you up with peace, so that your
believing lives, filled with the life-giving energy
of the Holy Spirit, will brim over with hope!*
Romans 15:13 The Message

covered

There's nothing like getting caught in the middle of a tornado to understand the importance of protection. This was the case for me a couple years ago. Granted, it was an EF-0 tornado—the mildest kind and, thankfully, no one was hurt. But to me, any weather event that ends in the word "tornado" gets my attention.

At the time, Jay and I were out running errands. The weather app on my phone was screaming, "Seek shelter now." As we sat at a stoplight watching the storm unfold, the rain started blowing sideways—an important clue we were at the wrong place at the wrong time.

Fortunately, we found shelter under a nearby bridge, which provided our only source of protection at this point. From our covered spot, we sat and watched as things that shouldn't be flying were lofted into the air at rapid speed.

Almost as quickly as the scene unfolded, it quieted. The sun came out and highlighted some amazing cloud formations that, in addition to providing a photo opportunity, underscored the magnitude of the storm. As we headed home relieved, we noticed moderate destruction just a stone's throw away from where we had parked.

I landed in an immediate space of gratitude, thanking God for his protection from the storm. In that moment, I also realized what a wonderful picture this experience painted of God's love and protection in our lives—not only in the storms we see but also in shielding us from storms unseen.

Friends, God has us covered! Even when life is swirling around and the rain is blowing sideways, he holds our future tightly in his hands. We never know when God's perceived "no" or "wait" is his protection for our lives, or part of his plan for gently carrying us to the next season with as few storms as possible.

We can experience a whole new level of freedom and peace when we stop measuring God's love through our storms, and instead view our storms through the lens of his unfailing love for us. When we choose to root down in the truth of God's love, we can rise up restored!

test it

———————————○———————————

God's protection is often seen in hindsight.

Think back over your life to something you absolutely had to have at the time that did not come to pass. How could that have been God's shelter for you? How can viewing future situations through the lens of God's protection change your perspective and allow you to practice trusting him more? Take a moment and spend some time in gratitude, thanking God for guarding your life in the seen and the unseen.

my notes

_____

_____

_____

_____

_____

_____

_____

_____

_____

trust it

Whoever dwells in the shelter of the Most High will rest in the shadow of the Almighty. I will say of the LORD, "He is my refuge and my fortress, my God, in whom I trust.

Psalm 91:1 – 2

father knows best

LIVE LOVED

Nine years ago, I lost my dad to a courageous battle with cancer. I miss him terribly. Dad was a selfless, quiet, and gentle man known for his sweet and cheerful smile. Some of my fondest memories are the simple things we did together, like going to the car wash when I was a kid, or taking walks in the park as adults when we happened to be unemployed at the same time.

Of course, I also appreciated the life lessons I learned from Dad.

For one, he taught me the value of perseverance. Case in point: In 1974, the St. Louis Cardinal's second baseman, Lou Brock, was closing in on his attempt to break Maury Wills' stolen base record. Dad and I went to Busch Stadium every night during that particular home series until Lou broke the record, just so we could be there to see it. And we did! I remember that night like it was yesterday, and I still have the "Lou Lou Lou" t-shirt I bought to commemorate the occasion.

Dad also taught me how to be flexible, as we'd often go on vacation without having hotel reservations in advance. Can you imagine that—no TripAdvisor? Well, we lived it. We'd show up to a destination and then find a place to stay. I remember being frustrated about this when I was a kid (obviously, my default need to have everything figured out started early.) But it worked out. Maybe not to our level of ideal, but we always had a place to lay our head and great stories about the more "interesting" spots we landed—the cabin in the middle of a horse pasture being one of my favorites.

Thankfully, Mom is still living and we often have a chance to reminisce about the life lessons from Dad. While all have a mark on my tapestry, one of the most important lessons I learned from both Dad and Mom is this: God loves me.

God. Loves. Me.

And it's not love like I love sunsets on the beach. Or I love cross country skiing in the Colorado snow. Or I love spending time with Jay and Weaver, our Golden Retriever.

It's a love deeper than I can possibly fathom. There are no limits, no boundaries, no conditions. There is nothing—*no* thing—I can do to cause God to love me less. And there is nothing I can do to make him love me more. God deliberately chooses to love me where I am, for who I am...mistakes and all. Even on the days when I am not being mindful to run with him, he is always running with me.

I don't know where you are in your faith walk—whether you've ever considered the magnitude of God's love for you or if you've experienced it firsthand. But wherever you are, know this: learning to *live loved* as you are by God will ignite your deliberate journey and fuel your desire to get to know him more.

Extravagant. Unconditional. Eternal. Love. When you are touched by it, you are changed.

rest

*I pray that out of his glorious
riches he may strengthen you with
power through his Spirit in your
inner being, so that Christ may dwell
in your hearts through faith. And
I pray that you, being rooted and
established in love, may have power,
together with all the Lord's holy
people, to grasp how wide and long
and high and deep is the love of
Christ, and to know this love that
surpasses knowledge--that you
may be filled to the measure of
all the fullness of God.*
Ephesians 3:16 – 19

grow deeper with God

- God is always in control, even on your worst days. He doesn't ask you to get all cleaned up to have a relationship with him. He loves you as you are, where you are.

- Your identity as a beloved child of God is the only one that will remain unchanged through shifting seasons. Life's labels limit you, but God's love for you is limitless.

- Being intentional to know God on a deeper level is at the heart of your practice to live more deliberately. Feeding your faith will ultimately strengthen your trust.

- God himself is hope. Be audacious to get your hopes up and dream with God. Hope expectantly and keep the faith!

- Stop measuring God's love through the storms in your life and instead view your storms through the lens of his unfailing love and compassion for you.

- God deliberately created you to love you. Learning to live loved as you are by God will ignite your deliberate journey and fuel your desire to get to know him more.

sending forth

———————◦———————

MY PRAYER FOR YOUR CONTINUING JOURNEY

This is not the end, Tribe. Today is the first day of the rest of your *deliberate* life! Go for it and grow through it. It's a process, not a perfect. You. Can. Do. This. Be persistent. Be patient. Be positive. And, most of all, be prayerful.

In the perfect world, which (of course) we know doesn't exist, I'd be there to join hands with you at this very moment and pray over your journey going forward. Who knows, maybe someday we'll get to do that together! In the meantime, I hope you will read and receive this prayer from my heart.

In fact, why not get a little crazy? I give you permission to tear out these two pages, carry them with you, and read this prayer when you need a little encouragement. *Deliberately.*

To the amazing person reading *deliberate*:

I pray you find a new level of trust, awe, and surrender in your faith journey as you walk out the narrow path of *deliberate*.

I pray you begin to seek God's wisdom more intentionally as you live out the adventurous life he has designed especially for you.

I pray you more fully receive God's unconditional love and learn to see yourself through his grace-filled eyes... knowing God made you in his image, for his joy, and he has some awesome plans for you.

I pray you stand confidently on the promise that what's impossible with man *is* possible with God. That you live courageously knowing thateven when you don't understand the "why" behind the "what"—God is in control. He is for you. He will work everything together for good.

I pray you develop a deep sense of self-compassion. That you nurture the positives in your life, and the negatives no longer have a stronghold on you. That you learn to care for yourself so you can care for others out of fullness rather than depletion.

I pray that you will become more comfortable living in the mystery of *not* having things figured out. I pray you will be strong yet you will learn to be still. That you will be courageous yet allow God to strengthen you in weakness. That you will stay motivated yet stay patient. That you will move your feet confidently towards greater authenticity in your own skin, in your current season, as God masterfully created you.

I pray that as you practice refocusing on God and his truth—and as you practice releasing hindrances like fear, perfection, and control—that your life balance, boundaries, and priorities will be restored...and that you will experience the lavish freedom that comes from unleashing extreme trust in God. One decision at a time.

Amen!

Tribe, I encourage you to live lightly. Believe boldly. Pray continually.
And don't forget to breathe.

Kathy

rest

The faithful love of the Lord never ends!
His mercies never cease.
Great is his faithfulness; his mercies
begin afresh each morning.
I say to myself, "The Lord is
my inheritance; therefore
I will hope in him!"
Lamentations 3:22-24 NLT

acknowledgments

The tapestry of *deliberate* was woven over many years, through countless life experiences and with a lot of encouragement along the way. In the perfect world, I would write a flawless list of acknowledgments capturing every single person who has been part of this tapestry. However, I will make peace with imperfection. I'll do my best to capture those who have contributed to the hands-on process of bringing the book to reality as well as those who have left the greatest fingerprints on recent seasons of my faith journey.

To my husband, Jay: You are my soul mate and my biggest cheerleader. You ground me, you speak truth to me, and you have loved me unconditionally through the most challenging times in life and in my career. Thank you for believing in *deliberate* and standing strong to the finish line. I'm grateful for your Godly leadership in our home and feel incredibly blessed we get to do life together. I love your sense of humor and you are my favorite person in the whole world to spend time with. I look forward to our next adventure!

To my Mom: The whole process of organizing the manuscript began with you. Thank you not only for your joyful encouragement, but for printing out almost every one of my "Narrow Gate Nuggets" since I began writing them in 2011. That red notebook full of nuggets is what helped me hit the ground running when I got serious about rewriting them for *deliberate*.

To Sharon Graham: You might be surprised to see your name in a book you didn't even know I was writing. It's been awhile since our paths have crossed. But as I reflect on the tapestry of my faith walk, it was during my business coaching sessions with you in the mid-2000s that I turned an important corner in overcoming the overwhelm. Not only did you hold me accountable for taking baby steps to make changes, you spoke bold truth into my life about the extravagant, unconditional love of Jesus. Thank you.

To Stephanie Haynes: We met in the boxing gym, but it wasn't about the boxing. God had bigger plans. Hands down, this book would be nothing more than an idea without you in my life. Thank you for the invitation to be championed by Relevant Pages Press (which rocks, by the way). Throughout the process, you've had an incredible ability to be supportive and encouraging while at the same time giving me a good kick in the rear when I needed it. You are a mentor, a coach, and a precious friend.

To Bailey Kinney, Betts Keating, Dana Frazeur, Glory Castello, Jennifer Tubbiolo, and Stephanie Bernotas: Thank you for coming alongside and surrounding me with your amazing talent, positive energy, and valuable knowledge. You each brought something unique and meaningful to the process. I'm grateful God flowed all of you into my life because there is no way I could have assembled a team of this much creative awesomeness in my own strength.

To the advisory team and the inaugural members of deliberate Tribe: You are far more than the beta readers of a rough draft manuscript. You are encouragers, constructive critics, and—most of all—friends. Thank you for sharing your time, your hearts, your suggestions, and your honest (and sometimes hilarious) stories of why you crave the deliberate life. On days when I was discouraged with the writing process, your enthusiasm and support kept me going.

To the launch team: Your willingness to jump in and jump-start the sharing of *deliberate* was priceless. I appreciate the time and energy you invested to communicate about this book within your circles of influence. You were the first official "fans" of *deliberate*. I am humbled by your support and blessed by your friendship.

To the Narrow Gate community: *deliberate* is an offshoot of the Narrow Gate Nuggets I started writing in 2011. Your faithfulness to read them and encourage me is what fueled my faithfulness to keep writing. So many of you have touched my life I don't know where to begin. Even though Narrow Gate Wellness is in a quieter place for now, know that I will always hold a special place for you in my heart. I hope you will continue the journey with the *deliberate* Tribe.

To my family, friends, and prayer warriors: You have walked with me quietly behind the scenes and I value you beyond words. Even if you did not touch the book process directly, know that you touch my life deeply. That matters. A lot.

To the teachers, preachers, and authors who have shaped my faith journey: Thank you for telling your stories, sharing your struggles and speaking powerfully about your faith. Thank you for helping me know God better and for igniting my desire to go deeper. Especially to the pastors at our current church home: thank you for teaching truth from the Bible, for cultivating a culture of prayer, and for shepherding a space where an imperfect person like me can truly experience the amazing freedom that comes from doing life with Jesus.

I love you Jesus with all my heart. Thank you for breathing deliberate *into my mind, body, and soul.*

notes

1. "Deliberate - Definition of Deliberate in English," Oxford Dictionaries, accessed August 18, 2017, https://en.oxforddictionaries.com/definition/deliberate.

2. *Seinfeld,* season 5, episode 22, "The Opposite," directed by Tom Cherones, originally aired May 19, 1994, on NBC.

3. Mary Kutheis, "Typos, if any, are here to make you feel good about finding them. You're welcome," *The Better Path* (2004).

4. John Ortberg, "Ruthlessly Eliminate Hurry," *CT Pastors* (July 2002): accessed August 17, 2017, http://www.christianitytoday.com/pastors/2002/july-online-only/cln20704.html.

5. John Ortberg, *The Life You've Always Wanted: Spiritual Disciplines for Ordinary People* (Grand Rapids, MI: Zondervan, 2002), 77.

6. Headlines & Global News, "Average Person Checks Their IPhone or Other Smartphone Device HOW Many Times a Day?" Headlines & Global News, October 08, 2013, accessed September 01, 2017, http://www.hngn.com/articles/14376/20131008/average-person-checks-iphone-smartphone-device-many-times-day.htm.

7. Ruth Haley Barton, *Sacred Rhythms: Arranging Our Lives for Spiritual Transformation,* (Downers Grove, IL: InterVarsity Press, 2006), 36.

8. Stephanie Haynes, "Who God says you are," *Stephanie Haynes Consulting Newsletter* (April 20, 2017).

about the author

Kathy Broska is a wellness enthusiast, travel buff, mindful bed-maker, and native Missourian with aspirations toward the Colorado mountains. For nearly 30 years, she has served in various corporate and strategic communication roles, most recently as a consultant helping global organizations effectively communicate during leadership transitions, major financial transactions, and mission-critical events.

In *deliberate*, Kathy makes a leap from speech writer and communication strategist to author. Through lessons learned during an overwhelming season of her consulting career, God ignited her passion to break the pattern of busyness so prevalent in our culture, and ultimately share her experiences in hopes of helping others to do the same.

A self-professed recovering perfectionist, Kathy has learned to refocus on what matters, release what doesn't, and find restoration in the only thing that truly satisfies: doing life with Jesus. In her spare time, she loves hanging out with her closest *deliberate* Tribe members: her amazing husband Jay and their beloved golden retriever Weaver.

For more information and to connect with the *deliberate* Tribe, visit www.deliberatetribe.com.

Made in the
USA
Columbia, SC